FAMOUS AMERICANS

IN

WORLD WAR II

A PICTORIAL HISTORY

By

William Van Osdol, Ph.D.

PHALANX
Publishing Co., Ltd.
1051 Marie Avenue
St. Paul, MN 55118 U.S.A.
612/454-0607

ISBN: 1-883809-06-1

Library of Congress Number: 94-073941

Text by: William Van Osdol, Ph.D.

Edited by: John Lambert

Cover Illustration by: John Valo

Cover Photos: Front cover, clockwise, top, John F. Kennedy, Joe DeMaggio, Clark Gable. Back cover, clockwise, top, Mickey Rooney (center) and unknown airmen, Bob Hope and Frances Langford, Ronald Reagan.

Published by:

Phalanx Publishing Co., Ltd.
1051 Marie Avenue West
St. Paul, MN 55118-4131 USA

INTRODUCTION

This work describes the WWII experience of 106 Americans whose names were prominent before the war or who came to prominence later.

It does not purport to be a complete study of all celebrities. Of the many who served with honor, information on military duty was lacking for some or, in a few cases, essential data was refused.

Of the thousands of civilians who selflessly gave their time to the United Service Organization (USO) only two are highlighted, Bob Hope and Joe E. Brown. Their dedication and tireless efforts were unique.

We salute these well known people and all the rest who rallied to the nation's defense in World War II.

DEDICATION

To my uncle, James Earl Van Osdol, killed in action, World War I.

To my late brother, James, who served aboard APA-118, U.S. Navy, World War II.

And to all those who honorably served their nation in World War II.

GENERAL HAP ARNOLD

Henry H. "Hap" Arnold commanded the United States Army Air Force in World War II. A 1907 graduate of West Point, he became a pioneer aviator in the fledgling air service of the U.S. Army.

General Hap Arnold, Commanding the Army Air Force in WW II. (Credit: USAF)

His early achievements in long distance flight, in establishing the Air Mail Service and his defense of Brigadier General Billy Mitchell, put him in the public eye during the 1930s. A strong advocate of air power he was appointed assistant chief of the Air Corps in 1936 and became chief of the air staff in 1938. In the years immediately preceding World War II Arnold worked diligently with the aviation industry to assure increased aircraft production. He was also an advocate of strategic bombing, a concept that would not be readily understood until the war broke.

His Army Air Force became the mightiest in history during World War II. The personnel and pilot training programs he supervised were responsible for the growth of personnel from 21,000 in 1935 to over two million in 1944. U.S. aircraft production skyrocketed from just 6,000 in 1940 to an incredible 262,000 in 1944. Arnold's efforts not only served the Air Force but fed thousands of aircraft to Allied nations.

In 1945 Arnold won his fourth star and became a five star general as the U.S. Air Force became an independent military branch. He died in 1950.

General Hap Arnold decorates some of his fighter pilots on Iwo Jima, June 1945. (Credit: USAF)

GENE AUTRY

Born Orvon Gene Autry on a Texas ranch in 1907 he sang for his own pleasure as a young man when Will Rogers happened to hear him and encouraged him to go into show business.

He began his career on radio and made several recordings which led to a small singing role in a 1934 Ken Maynard movie. A series, **Phantom Empire**, followed in thirteen parts, then came Autry's first starring role in the 1935 western, **Tumblin Tumbleweeds**. He went on to appear in many Republic Pictures "oaters" with his horse Champion and the inimitable comic sidekick Smiley Burnette. These popular movies made him one of the top box office stars and one of the top money makers of his day.

Although he had earned $600,000 in 1941, he applied for flight training in the Army Air Force and prepared himself with private flying lessons until called in July 1942. After attaining the rank of flight officer he was assigned to ferry supplies over the "Hump", the Himalayas air route from India to China that was notorious for its perils and treacherous weather. He was honorably discharged late in 1945.

Returning to Hollywood after the war, Autry made only ten more of his classic brand of western, most in 1953. Collectively he made 93 westerns and countless recordings. In 1978 he wrote an autobiography, **Back in the Saddle Again**.

But his greatest success was as a businessman. Autry formed his own film production company, a radio and TV chain, invested in oil and real estate, and publishing. These ventures caused him to drop from the public eye until he resurfaced as the owner of the California Angels American League baseball team.

Upper Right:
Cowboy movie favorite Gene Autry aboard Champion. (Credit: Gene Autry)

Left:
Gene Autry in the cockpit of a P-36 during his Air Force training. (Credit: Gene Autry)

LEW AYRES

A movie poster advertising Lew Ayres most famous role. (Credit: Film Favorites)

Born in Minneapolis, Minnesota in 1908, Ayres was a musician playing in a Hollywood night club in 1928 when a film executive asked him to take a screen test.

He was acting opposite famed Greta Garbo within one year. In 1930 he won international acclaim

A movie poster depicting Lew Ayres in one of his Dr. Kildare roles. (Credit: Film Favorites)

for his portrayal of a German soldier in **All Quiet on the Western Front**, the anti-war movie of its day.

Ayers appeared in almost 50 additional movies over the next decade, few of them matching his early success. Nine of them cast him in the role of a benign physician, the "Doctor Kildare" series. However, he was nominated for an Academy award for the 1948 film **Johnny Belinda.**

As a conscientious objector he refused to fight in World War II and saw his popularity fade and screen connections disappear. He volunteered for non-combatant medial duty and distinguished himself under fire in the Philippines in 1944.

Returning to Hollywood he made only fifteen more movies until 1978 before involving himself in the production of spiritual documentaries and working with UNESCO. Some of those later films were box office hits: **Advise and Consent, The Carpetbaggers, Battle For the Planet of the Apes, Damien,** and in 1978, **Battlestar Galactica**.

LLOYD BENTSEN

He was born in Mission, Texas on February 11, 1921 and attended the University of Texas achieving a law degree in 1942 just before enlisting in the Army. He married Edna Ruth Colbath in 1943.

Bentsen was selected for pilot training, won his wings and commission and after further training was sent overseas to Italy. He was a pilot in the 717th Bomb Squadron, 449th Bomb Group flying B-24 Liberator four-engined bombers from a base near the Italian heel. Late in his combat tour he rose to command his squadron.

During his missions over German occupied Europe Bentsen had a crash landing and a bizarre experience. Leading his unit on a mission to Vienna, Austria, his plane was hit by heavy anti-aircraft fire that resulted in the loss of power on two engines. His aircraft plunged out of control and after a successful struggle to right it he had lost several thousand feet of precious altitude. Knowing with some certainty that they would not make it back to an Allied Italian base and not wanting to ditch in the cold Adriatic (it was February 1944), Bentsen elected to try an emergency landing on the Island of Viz, a spot of supposed Guerrilla held territory with a landing strip off the coast of German held Yugoslavia.

With the help of his navigator Viz was located but with a low approach and lack of power the nose gear was crushed on landing and the plane slid to a stop on its nose. A swarm of heavily armed guerrillas, many of them women, approached the wreckage, and searching through the crowd an apprehensive Bentsen thought he saw a familiar face.

"Don't I know you?" Bentsen asked.

Capt. Lloyd Bentsen stands next to his B-24 Liberator in Italy during WW II. (Credit: Lloyd Bentsen)

Lloyd Bentsen's B-24 sits ingloriously on its nose on the remote island of Viz, but his crew members, glad to be alive, strike a jaunty pose. (Credit: Lloyd Bentsen)

"Sure, you're Lloyd Bentsen. I used to sack groceries for your mother when she went to the store in McAllen."

Reflecting on the astonishing meeting, Bentsen said, "I can't remember when I was happier to see a fellow from home."

Lloyd Bentsen went home a Major with the Distinguished Flying Cross and the Air Medal with three clusters. He retired from the Air Force reserve some years later with the rank of colonel.

He returned to the practice of law in McAllen, Texas until 1948 when he was appointed to a County Judgeship. He was then elected to Congress for two years, but returned to business interests in Texas. In 1971 he won election to the Senate of the United States,

remaining until 1993. He ran for the vice presidency in 1988 and gained a great deal of public exposure during the TV debates associated with that campaign.

He left the Senate to become Secretary of the Treasury under the Clinton Administration in 1993 and resigned from that post to return to Texas business interests in January 1995.

Editor's Note: George McGovern, found elsewhere in this volume, also made an emergency landing on the Island of Viz.

DICK BONG

Major Richard I. Bong in the cockpit of his Lockheed P-38 fighter in April 1944. (Credit: Campbell Archives)

Born in Poplar, Wisconsin on September 24, 1920 this farm boy became the most celebrated airman of World War II with the possible exception of Jimmy Doolittle.

As a lad he had a burning interest in aviation and joined the Army Aviation Cadet program. After winning his wings and commission he was dispatched to the Soutwest Pacific and assigned as a fighter pilot with the 9th Fighter Squadron, 49th Fighter Group in December 1942. Flying the P-38 Lightning over New Guinea and the Admiralty Islands, he soon became renowned for his skill as a pilot. He was an ace (five kills) by August 1943 and had increased his score to 21 by the time he was sent home on leave in November 1943.

A pair of aces, Dick Bong (left) and Tom McGuire, talk shop. Bong scored 40 aerial victories and McGuire 38. The latter was killed in action over the Philippines on January 7, 1945. (Credit McGuire AFB Archives)

Major Dick Bong shortly after being presented with the Medal of Honor by Gen. Douglas MacArthur. (Credit: Campbell Archives)

Volunteering for a second combat tour, he returned to the Pacific in February 1944. Although assigned to Fifth Fighter Command he continued flying combat missions, most frequently with his old unit, and continued knocking down enemy aircraft. He had soon surpassed Eddie Rickenbacker's World War I record of 26 victories when he was ordered home again. This time he took a gunnery refresher course, though none seem needed, and returned to the Pacific in October.

The newspapers never tired of reporting his victories and war correspondents delighted in chatting with the quiet, introverted man who was such a terror in the sky. These reports made his name a household word with the World War II generation.

Dick Bong kept his scoreboard of victories over Japanese aircraft painted on the side of his P-38 Lightning. (Credit: Campbell Archives)

Flying long range missions to the Dutch East Indies and then ranging into the Philippines he brought his score to 40 confirmed kills, eight probables and seven damaged by December 1944. At that point he was ordered withdrawn from combat and again returned home. He was awarded the Medal of Honor, pinned on him by General Douglas MacArthur, to go with a mass of additional decorations. He returned to Wisconsin, the acclamation of a nation and married his sweetheart, Marge.

With the war just days from being over and ensconsed in the seemingly safe job of test pilot at Lochheed Aircraft in California, Major Dick Bong was killed in the flame out of a P-80 Shooting Star jet. He bailed out but was too low for his parachute to open. He was buried with full military honors in Poplar.

His record of forty aerial victories has never been exceeded by an American flyer.

RICHARD BOONE

Born in Los Angeles in 1916, he attended Stanford University, then left to work in the oil fields, then tried boxing, house painting and writing as means of livelihood.

When World War II developed he enlisted in the U.S. Navy. After training he was assigned as an ordinance man to the aircraft carrier *Enterprise* and served through some of the early campaigns of the Pacific war. He returned to the States and won a berth as a radio-gunner and returned to the later stages of the Pacific war as a crew member in a TBF Avenger torpedo bomber.

Returning from the war, he used his GI Bill to prepare for the stage and made his Broadway debut in the 1947 version of "Medea". This effort ultimately brought him a movie offer and he appeared in **The Halls of Montezuma** in 1951.

Richard Boone (Credit: The Academy of Motion Picture Arts and Sciences)

His craggy face and gravely voice made him a heavy, either of the good or bad variety, but always he appeared in adventure roles, mostly westerns. Some of his movies were: **Siege at Red River** (1954), **Man Without a Star** (1955), **Away All Boats** (1956), **The Alamo** (1960), **Rio Conchos** (1964), **Hombre** (1967), **The Arrangement** (1969), **Big Jake** (1971), **The Shootist** (1976) and **The Big Sleep** (1978). He appeared in 42 movies, the last in 1979.

However, much of his popularity stemmed from television. He starred in "Medic" and the long running "Have Gun Will Travel" as a black rigged gun fighter who only shot the bad guys. Later he produced "The Richard Boone Show".

Boone died of cancer in 1981.

ERNEST BORGNINE

Born Ermes Effron Borgnino, in 1917 in Hamden, Connecticut to Italian parents, Ernest lived both in Italy and the U.S. in his youth.

He joined the U.S. Navy in 1935 as an apprentice seaman and spent 10 years in the service serving, largely on destroyers, as a gunner's mate during World War II.

After his honorable discharge he studied acting at the Randall School of Dramatic Art in Hartford, then worked with a Virginia theatrical group.

After some TV appearances, he had a part in **China Corsairs** (1951), his first movie and made two more that year. He was quickly type cast as a heavy for major roles in **The Stranger Wore a Gun, From Here to Eternity, Demetrius and the Gladiators, The Bounty Hunter, Vera Cruz** and **Bad Day at Black Rock**. Then in a complete character turnabout he played a shy, lovable lug in the 1955 movie **Marty** and won an Academy Award as best actor. Additional honors came from the New York Film Critics Award, the National Board of Review and the Cannes Film Festival.

Many movie rolls followed generally westerns, period pieces, and war movies, all adding to Borgnine's loyal following of fans. Yet his greatest public success was in TV comedy. After a 1964 feature film, **McHale's Navy**, he began a long running TV series (reruns continue today) of **McHale's Navy** that co-starred Tim Conway and Joe Flynn. He was featured in another TV series, **Air Wolf**, that ran from 1984 to 1986.

Borgnine has made over 40 movies including several filmed in Italy, Canada, and England. A few of his more memorable are: **The Vikings** (1957), **The Flight of the Phoenix** (1965), **The Wild Bunch** (1969), **The Poseidon Adventure** (1972), **The Greatest** (1977), **Young Warriors** (1983) and most recently, **Mistress** (1992).

Ernest Borgnine (left) and cast members Tim Conway and Joe Flynn from the hit TV comedy series, *McHale's Navy*. (Credit: Film Favorites)

MARGARET BOURKE-WHITE

One of the world's foremost photo-journalists was born on June 14, 1906 in New Jersey.

She worked for newspapers and for Time, Life, Fortune magazines. Henry Luce hired her as part of the original staff of Life magazine after seeing her 1930 photos of Russia, the drought ridden plains in 1934 and poignant pictures of Southern share croppers. One of Life's most memorable covers is her photo of the concrete columns of the Fort Peck Dam during its 1936 construction.

In 1940 she married novelist Erskine Caldwell who traveled with her for a time. She traveled widely in the Canadian Arctic, took pictures of the New York skyline from dizzying heights. In 1941 she traveled back to Russia via China, and was present in Moscow when the Germans attacked Russia. Returning to the U.S. she sailed in an armed convoy from Archangel to London.

Margaret Bourke-White in full high altitude flight gear, camera in hand, climbs out of a B-17 bomber. (Credit: Margaret Bourke-White, Life Magazine, Time Inc.)

As the United States entered World War II she received Pentagon accreditation as the only female war correspondent and flew to England in 1942. To cover the invasion of North Africa she sailed on a troop ship from England. It was torpedoed and sunk by a German U-boat off Algeria and Margaret took to a life boat with other passengers and crew, saving one camera and the clothes on her back.

Preparing to cover the North African air war she was bombed by German planes in Biskra, then wrangled Maj. Gen. Jimmy Doolittle's permission to fly on a combat mission. She went in a B-17 bomber with a formation of the 97th Bomb Group raiding Tunis airfields.

Through all of her adventures Margaret took stunning photos that seemed to be of studio quality.

Returning to the war, she went to Italy and saw the battle for the Rome-Arno line. She again wrangled a flight over the lines in the area of Cassino to take astounding photos of the battle front. On the ground she was shelled by German artillery.

Shifting her focus to Northern Europe and the Western Front she joined Patton's Third Army on its dash across the Rhine in the Spring of 1945. When Patton's forces entered Buchenwald and beheld the horrors of that death camp she was there to take photos that gave stark reality to what had only been rumored.

In the postwar period she was present for the partition of Imperial India into two independent nations, and was nearby when Gandhi was assassinated.

She covered the Korean war and toured South Africa. In her lifetime she photographed every great statesman or world leader. Along the way she wrote seven books on what she had witnessed, three of them in conjunction with Erskine Caldwell.

She contracted Parkinson's Disease in the 60s and documented the ravages of that illness as she fought it in a long and heroic struggle. She died on August 27, 1971.

PAPPY BOYINGTON

Born Gregory Boyington on December 4, 1912 in Coeur d'Alene, Idaho, he joined the U.S. Marines in 1936 and became an aviator.

Shortly before the start of World War II General Claire Chennault, was recruiting American service pilots to volunteer for his Chinese mercenary air unit, called the American Volunteer Group, and popularized with the name "Flying Tigers." Boyington left the Marines (a leave of absence) to join Chennault's group, the pay and bonus plan (for Japanese aircraft victories) being a fortune for that time. In a relatively short time he became an ace with the Flying Tigers, but had differences with the command structure and returned to the United States.

Rejoining the Marine Corps he was first relegated to administrative duties because of a leg injury. By mid-1943 he had talked his way to the Pacific, beseeching the Corps for command of a fighter unit. They thought him too old for fighters at 32, and after years in the Corps he had developed a reputation

Margaret Bourke-White interviewing P-38 ace Lt. Jack Ilfrey, 1st Fighter Group, in North Africa. (Credit: Jack Ilfrey)

as being brash and belligerent. However, Major Boyington persisted and put together a unit of some misfits from other squadrons at Espiritu Santo, and because the need was great, his squadron was formally recognized (VMF-214) and supplied with Vought F4U Corsairs. His young pilots called him "Pappy".

Regardless of age or disposition, Boyington proved to be a superb pilot and an extraordinary leader. With his self-named "Black Sheep" he became the scourge of the Northern Solomon Islands. In four months his squadron downed 120 Japanese aircraft, with Boyington bagging nineteen himself. On January 3, 1944 in a vicious dogfight over the Japanese main base of Rabaul, Boyington and his wingman were both seen to go down.

His fate remained unknown until the end of the war, but Boyington survived a parachute jump, random beatings and seventeen months of imprisonment. When released from a Japanese prison camp at the end of the war, he was awarded the Medal of Honor and the Navy Cross that had been earned in the Solomons. Based on the three kills he got just before being shot down he ran his string of victories to 28, highest in the Marine Corps for World War II.

However, his greatest achievement may have been the tenacity and will to survive that he displayed in P.O.W. camps. Countless American captives credited Boyington with giving them the will to live and withstand the tortuous Japanese treatment.

He retired from the Marines in 1947 with the rank of colonel. Divorced and remarried, he worked at odd jobs, wrote his autobiography, "Baa, Baa Black

Major Gregory "Pappy" Boyington (left) leader of VMF-214 in the Solomons. (Credit: Campbell Archives)

Sheep", in 1958, made personal appearances, and battled alcoholism. In the 1970s he was technical adviser to a television show that was built around the story of his character and the Black Sheep. Robert Conrad played Boyington in the one-hour series that ran from 1976 to 1978.

Pappy Boyington died of cancer on January 11, 1988 in Fresno, California.

Pappy Boyington and his "Black Sheep" flew the Chance Vought F4U Corsair in combat against the Japanese. (Credit: Lambert Archives)

CHARLES BRONSON

Born Charles Bunchinsky in Ehrenfeld, Pennsylvania in 1920, he was one of fifteen children of a coal miner. He too worked the mines of Pennsylvania.

He enlisted in the U.S. Army Air Force in World War II and after schooling became a tail gunner on a B-29. He was sent to the Pacific where he completed 25 combat missions.

Returning from the war he studied art and joined a repertory company as a set designer. That eventually led him into movie roles, usually as a tough guy, his rugged features and strong physique making him ideal for such parts.

His first movie role was in 1951 and since then he has appeared in some 70, many of them classic westerns. He has also made films in Mexico, France, Italy and England. Some of his movies are: **Red Skies of Montana** (1952), **Run of the Arrow** (1957), **The Magnificent Seven** (1960), **Kid Galahad** (1962),**Battle of the Bulge** (1967), **Once Upon a Time in the West** (1968), **The Valachi Papers** (1972), **Death Wish** (1974), **Breakheart Pass** (1976), **The Evil that Men Do** (1984), and **The Indian Runner** (1991).

In 1971 he received a Golden Globe Award as the worlds's most popular actor. Bronson appeared in very limited television. He was in several movies with his second wife, the late Jill Ireland. He has seven children.

JOE E. BROWN

Joe Evans Brown was born in 1892 in Holgate, Ohio. A circus acrobat at nine, he played semi-pro baseball and performed in vaudeville and burlesque before reaching Broadway in 1918.

He first brought his elastic face and slapstick style of comedy to the screen in 1928 and gained wide popularity as one of the nations enduring funny men in a string of comedy farces.

He had largely retired from the screen at the outbreak of World War II, and although too old to serve

Joe E. Brown in AAF high altitude flight jacket in Europe. (Credit:: Van Osdol Archives)

Charles Bronson (standing right) in a scene from the movie *The Great Escape*. (Credit: Film Favorites)

Joe E. Brown with his patented grin, strikes a pose while visiting an Air Force base in China. (Credit: Campbell Archives)

at 50 he readily volunteered his services to entertain troops. Thousands of show business people participated in the USO programs, but none (except Bob Hope) traveled as far and wide as Joe E. Brown.

Appearing even in remote China, Europe and various Pacific islands, his infectious humor and broad smile made him a favorite. He continued his punishing tour throughout World War II despite his own personal loss. His son, Captain Don E. Brown, a flyer, was killed in action.

Joe E. Brown is the only known civilian to have received the Bronze Star Medal in World War II.

He acted only sparingly after the war but always in comic situations: **The Tender Years** (1947), **Show Boat** (1951), and **Some Like it Hot** (1959). He wrote an autobiography, **Laughter is a Wonderful Thing** in 1959.

He died in 1973.

GEORGE BUSH

Ens. George Bush in the cockpit of his Grumman TBM Avenger torpedo bomber. (Credit: Pensacola NAM)

Born in Milton Massachusetts on June 12 , 1924, George Herbert Walker Bush attended Phillips Academy in Andover, Massachusetts enlisting in the Navy's flight training program in 1942.

He won his Navy Gold Wings and his commission as ensign on 28 May 1943 and after advanced training was assigned to Torpedo Squadron 51 aboard the aircraft carrier, *San Jacinto*. At the age of 19, flying a TBM Avenger bomber he entered combat in the Central Pacific with his squadron. He flew 58 combat missions and was forced down twice.

The first instance was during the first Battle of the Philippine Sea in June 1944. While flying sub CAP over the fleet his engine failed and he was forced to ditch his plane in the water. He and his two crewmen were rescued by a destroyer from which they witnessed the savage air battle.

Just two months after his 20th birthday, on September 2, 1944, Lieutenant (j.g.) Bush was participating in an attack on radio installations on Chichi Jima, an island in the Bonin group, 600 miles

The Grumman Avenger bomber, largest carrier aircraft of its day. The one shown here was from Bush's squadron, VT-51. (Credit: Barrett Tillman)

Lt. (j.g.) George Bush in his third Avenger. All were named for his wife, Barbara. (Credit: US Naval Institute)

south of Japan. His plane was hit by anti-aircraft fire and with fire spreading he was forced to parachute. He was rescued from the Northern Pacific by the submarine *Finback*.

Bush was honorably discharged after the end of the war during which he had been awarded the Distinguished Flying Cross and the Air Medal with three oak leaf clusters.

He married his wartime sweetheart, Barbara, on January 6, 1945 and entered Yale University to complete his education. After graduation the Bush family moved to Texas where George achieved success in the oil business.

Entering politics in 1967 Bush won a seat in the U.S. House of Representatives from Texas and served until 1971 when he was chosen as Ambassador to China. Serving in China for four years, he was then tapped as Director of the CIA until 1977.

He served as Vice-President for two terms with Ronald Reagan and was elected the 41st President of the United States in 1988.

After being defeated for a second term in 1992 he returned to Texas where he and Barbara live in retirement.

President and Mrs. George Bush (Credit: Pres. Bush's office)

CLAIRE L. CHENNAULT

Born in Texas in 1890, he moved to Louisiana with his family after the death of his mother. His father became a cotton plantation manager.

He attended Louisiana State University and participated in its ROTC program and did some amateur boxing, but left to get a teaching degree form Louisiana State Normal School. He both taught and coached.

With the outbreak of World War I he enlisted in the Army and received a reserve commission in the Infantry, transferring to the Signal Corps and entering the air service. He learned to fly but too late for World War I combat. In April 1920 he received a permanent commission and saw service at air bases throughout the country. In 1923 he was given command of the 19th Pursuit Squadron at Wheeler Field, Oahu during a tour of duty in Hawaii.

During the next decade he gained some fame within the aviation fraternity as a pursuit expert, leader and innovator. He organized a team of stunt flyers who performed at the Cleveland Air Races in 1934-35. But promotions were slow in the peacetime Air Corps and he did not achieve the rank of major until 1936. By this

Brig. Gen. Claire Chennault (far right) and some of his 14th Air Force officers display their emblem in China 1943. (Credit: Lambert Archives)

time he had become hard of hearing from too many hours in open cockpit aircraft and decided to retire. He moved his wife Nell and eight children back to Louisiana.

In 1937 he was offered a job as consultant to the Chinese Air Force, already being invaded by Japan in the opening rounds of World War II. He assisted Chiang Kai-shek in assembling a rather motley collection of foreign aircraft, all the Chinese could afford, and set about training an indigenous air force. But his efforts were frustrated by the superiority of both Japan's aircraft and her airmen. Having achieved a rank of prominence in the Chinese Air Force, Chennault set about creating the funds and equipment to field a mercenary fighter unit.

That organization, labeled the American Volunteer Group, gathered pilots from the three military air services of the U.S. and with 100 Curtiss P-40B Tomahawk fighters became the famed "Flying Tigers." The unit did not go into combat until just about the time of the Pearl Harbor attack, but in the next six months of solid Allied reversals in Asia and the Pacific, the success of the Flying Tigers was one of the few bright spots. In July 1942 the U.S. established a military presence in China by creating the Fourteenth Air Force. Chennault was made its commander and given the rank of Brigadier General in the Army Air Force. His volunteer group was disbanded, most of the airmen returning to their prior organizations and many to combat. With the nucleus that remained, a tortuous supply line and meager resources, Chennault built the Fourteenth Air Force into a formidable fighting organization which he commanded until wars end.

He received his second star in 1943 and was made a lieutenant general after retirement in July 1958.

A dozen or more books on the subject of the China air war and the 1943 movie, **Flying Tigers**, starring John Wayne, have served to perpetuate and popularize General Chennault with successive generations. When the movie **God is My Co-Pilot** (1945) was adapted from the book of the same name, Chennault was further thrust into public view. He was played by Raymond Massey in the latter film.

Chennault moved to Formosa after the war and formed China National Airlines Corporation, a civil carrier operating in Southeast Asia. (Bob Prescott, a former Flying Tiger, organized a cargo carrying airline, "Flying Tiger Lines, Inc.", in the U.S.) Chennault sided with Chiang Kai-shek and the Nationals in the civil war that wracked the mainland. In 1947 he divorced his wife and married Anna Chan and subsequently had two children by her. He died on July 27, 1958.

Raymond Massey, seated second from the left, portrays Chennault in Scott's *God is My Co-Pilot*. (Credit: Film Favorites)

JACQUELINE COCHRAN

"Jackie" was one of America's preeminent women fliers and became such despite the most humble beginnings. She was born about 1910 in a squalid North Florida sawmill camp. She was orphaned as an infant and when eight adopted by a foster family in Columbus, Georgia.

As a child she worked a 12-hour shift in a cotton mill for pennies per hour. She later learned the beuticians trade and haircutting and moved to Montgomery, Alabama, and then to Pensacola. With grim determination she climbed the ladder working for a salon with shops in New York and Miami. This last move found her in occasional association with people of wealth, and one, Floyd Odlum, suggested that she could cover more territory by flying. In 1932 she took flying lessons at Roosevelt Field on Long Island and from the first lesson, she said, " the beauty operator ceased to exist and an aviator was born."

She drove cross country and entered the Ryan Flying School in San Diego where she got her commercial license. With her first airplane, a Travelaire, and a salon in Chicago she set up her own cosmetics business. She first entered air racing competition in 1935 and participated frequently in the Bendix Trophy

Jackie Cochran in the cockpit of a Curtiss P-40 fighter. She and her WASP comrades flew every type of Army Air Force aircraft during WW II. (Credit: USAF)

Jackie Cochran, Director of the WASPs and her boss, Gen. Hap Arnold. (Credit: The Dora Strother Collection at Texas Women's University)

race and making speed records, gaining national attention. Along the way she married Odlum in 1936. Starting in 1938 she won the Harmon Trophy race three years running as the world's outstanding women flier.

In World War II, she was granted a commission in the Air Force Reserve. She formed and led the unit known as the Women's Air Force Service Pilots (known as WASPs), an organization that took over the majority of the Air Force ferrying requirements, thus freeing hundreds of male pilots for combat service. Although the WASPs were disbanded at the end of World War II,

Cochran held her commission in the reserve until her retirement in 1970 with the rank of colonel.

In 1964 she became the fastest women aviatrix when she flew a jet fighter at 1,429 miles per hour, then she settled down from the flying business to manage her cosmetics company. Cochran died in Indio, California in 1980, and still holds more speed, altitude and distance records than any other pilot, male or female, in aviation history.

ROBERT CUMMINGS

Born in Joplin, Missouri in 1908, he attended Drury College and Carnegie Tech.

He began acting, literally, on Broadway in 1931 by using a fake British accent. He broke into films in the same way, using a thick southern drawl for **The Winning Ticket** in 1935.

Cummings appeared in many light romantic and comedy roles between 1936 and 1940: **Arizona Mahoney, Three Cheers for Love, College Swing, Rio, Charlie McCarthy Detective, It Started With Eve.**

He joined the Army Air Force in 1941, entered flight training, and after winning his wings was assigned as a flight instructor. He also did USO and bond tours.

He maintained his interest in flying after the war as he returned to making his usual brand of picture. However, he played some dramatic roles, the most notable being in **The Lost Moment** (1947) and **Dial M For Murder** (1954). His last movie was made in 1967, **Five Golden Dragons**.

Cumming's gained further public recognition in television with "The Bob Cummings Show", 1955 - 1962, and "My Living Doll", 1964-1965. He died in 1990.

TONY CURTIS

Born in 1925 in the Bronx, his name was Bernard Schwartz. Curtis was the son of an immigrant and grew up in poverty in a tough neighborhood. He first performed on a local stage in amateur productions. He attended Seward Park High School.

He joined the Navy in 1943 and after training was assigned to duty at Guam. Curtis was injured during a torpedo loading accident. After a period of hospitalization he returned to sea duty and sailed north on submarine tender *Proteus* to be present in Tokyo Bay for the Japanese surrender. He was honorably discharged in 1946.

Curtis returned to New York and studied at City College of New York and the New York Dramatic Workshop. His first acting job was with a stock company that toured the Catskills. After working in an off-Broadway show he headed for Hollywood and his good looks got him into movies in 1949.

He handled a variety of dramatic roles in the 1950s but found his greatest success in comedy in later years. He won an Oscar nomination for his performance in the 1958 film, **The Defiant Ones** and has performed in over 80 movies.

Bob Cummings and Priscilla Lane are clearly into heavy intrigue in this scene from the movie *Saboteur*. (Credit: Film Favorites)

Tony Curtis (swimming) in a scene from *Operation Petticoat*. (Credit: Film Favorites)

Some of his memorable movies are: **Flesh and Fury** (1952), **Houdini** (1953),**Six Bridges to Cross** (1955), **Trapeze** (1956), **The Sweet Smell of Success** (1957), **The Vikings** (1958), **Operation Petticoat** (1959), **Spartacus** (1960), **The List of Adrian Messenger** (1963), **Sex and the Single Girl** (1965), **Not With My Wife You Don't** (1966), **Suppose They Gave a War and Nobody Came** (1970), **Lepke** (1976), **The Last Tycoon** (1976), **Little Miss Marker** (1980) and **Prime Target** (1991).

Curtis has been married three times. His daughter (by actress Janet Leigh) is actress Jamie Lee Curtis. He is an accomplished painter and has tried his hand at fiction.

Tony Curtis (right) in his portrayal of Ira Hayes for the movie *The Outsider.* (Credit: Film Favorites)

JOE DIMAGGIO

Born in 1914 in Martinez, California, he would become one of the most famous and recognizable baseball players in American history.

He joined the New York Yankees as a rookie in 1936, and though he arrived in the shadow of the legendary Ruth and Gehrig became an instant star. He had a variety of nick names applied by the sports writers and reinforced by adoring fans: "Joltin' Joe", "The Bronx Bomber", "The Yankee Clipper".

Joe played for the Yankees until called by the services in 1943 and then he served in Special Service units as ordered. He was a member of the Army Air Force and also participated in bond drives until his honorable discharge in 1945.

He played with the Yankees for a total of thirteen years, retiring from baseball in 1951. His lifetime statistics are most impressive: a .325 batting average, 361 homeruns, ten World Series. A slugger of heroic proportions, he was also one of the most graceful outfielders who ever played the game. He was elected to the Baseball Hall of Fame in 1955.

His highly publicized marriage to movie star, Marilyn Monroe, in 1954 kept him in the public eye much longer than the marriage lasted.

Joe DiMaggio in his prime with a young "comer" Mickey Mantle. (Credit: Van Osdol Archives):

BOB DOLE

Born Robert J. Dole in Russell, Kansas on July 22, 1923, he attended the University of Kansas until military service intervened.

Entering the U.S. Army on June 1, 1943, Dole was sent to several training schools before applying for Officer Candidate School. He won his commission at Fort Benning, Georgia and was shipped to Italy and in February 1945 assigned to I Company, 3rd Battalion, 85th Regiment, 10th Mountain Division.

Dole received a minor wound in an action on March 18th. Then, just a month later while leading his platoon against entrenched Germans Dole's radioman was badly wounded. Second Lieutenant Dole reached the wounded man and joining him in a shell hole administered morphine. But Dole was then hit by an explosion that erupted under his right shoulder. Because of the intense fire fight the wounded could not be evacuated to a field hospital for nearly ten hours.

Recruit Bob Dole in 1943, shortly after joining the Army. (Credit: Dole archivist K. Dondanville)

A rough and ready band of soldiers are the men of "I" Company, 3rd Battalion, 85th Regiment. Lt. Bob Dole is hatless and kneeling at the far left. (Credit: Dole archivist K. Dondanville)

By the time Dole reached medical help all of his limbs were paralyzed and he was soon evacuated to Casablanca, Morocco for further treatment, then airlifted back to the States and finally sent to convalesce at Winter General Hospital, Topeka, Kansas.

It was something of a miracle that he lived and his recovery was slow. The explosion that put him out of the war had damaged his right shoulder, collarbone, large shoulder bone, cervical vertebra and spinal cord. Paralysis from the neck down had disrupted both bladder and bowel functions and Dole's weight had gone from 195 pounds down to just 120. He was under hospital care going through recovery then rehabilitation until 1947.

He was decorated with the Purple Heart and two clusters and the Bronze Star and two clusters.

Dole completed his education at The University of Arizona and Washburn University, Topeka, achieving a law degree in 1951 and gaining admission to the Kansas Bar in 1952. While practicing law in Russell, he won election to the Kansas House of Representatives and left that office to be Russell County Attorney. In 1969 he was elected to the U.S. House of Representatives and later the Senate of the United States and is today the Senate Majority leader.

He is married (for the second time) to Elizabeth Hanford, President of the American Red Cross.

Senator Bob Dole, Majority Leader, the U.S. Senate. He wears the Purple Heart ribbon in his lapel on all occasions. (Credit: Dole archivist K. Dondanville)

JIMMY DOOLITTLE

He was born in Alameda, California in 1896. He married his high school sweetheart, Josephine Daniels in 1917 and they had two sons, both Air Force officers.

"Jimmy" began his flying career with the Army Air Service in 1917. He pioneered cross-country flight in 1922 with a 24 hour transit of the U.S. He contributed in the development of many aviation instruments and made the first successful blind flight using instruments only.

He resigned from the Air Corps in 1930 to involve himself in civil aviation ventures and joined Shell Oil Company.

With World War II already underway in Europe and Asia, Doolittle returned to military service with the rank of major and was assigned the task of converting the auto industry to aircraft production.

Early in 1942, when Japanese forces seemed invincible and American morale was at low ebb, he helped concoct a plan to bomb Honshu. He trained several select crews and saw to the modification of the B-25 Mitchell twin-engined bomber for this undertaking. On April 18, 1942 he led his sixteen B-25s on the Japan raid, with an unprecedented takeoff from the deck of the aircraft carrier *Hornet*. Because the *Hornet* task force had run across a Japanese fishing boat before reaching the planned launch location, it was assumed that their presence had been disclosed. Thus the Doolittle bombers had a longer run to the target than planned. After bombing all of the planes were lost due to flak damage or lack of fuel. Most crash landed in China, one in Siberia. Only a handful of the crews were killed or taken prisoner, several of the latter executed by the Japanese. Doolittle thought the mission had been a failure and wondered if he would be court martialled.

But the presence of those bombers over Tokyo stunned the Japanese high command and gave Americans a much needed shot in the arm. Doolittle returned to undying fame and the award of the Medal of Honor from President Roosevelt. A lieutenant colonel at the time of the raid, Doolittle was jumped to

The Doolittle bombers lined up on the deck of carrier *Hornet* en route to their historic launching. (Credit: USAF via Norm Avery Collection)

Brig. Gen. Jimmy Doolittle in the pilot's seat of a B-25 Mitchell at the North American plant, Inglewood, CA, shortly after his epic raid on Honshu. (Credit: Norm Avery)

brigadier general and given command first of the Twelfth Air Force, then the Fifteenth (both in the Mediterranean theater) then the Northwest African Strategic Air Force. Not a desk leader, Doolittle flew 25 combat missions. In 1944 he assumed command of the Eighth Air Force in England then carrying out the strategic bombing of Germany.

With the end drawing near in Europe he went to the Pacific in 1945 to prepare the way for the transfer of the Eighth Air Force to that theatre of war. The dropping of the atom bombs obviated the exercise.

Doolittle returned to Shell Oil as an executive in 1946, but he continued to serve in a consulting capacity to the Air Force, and several other government boards and commissions.

He retired from the Air Force at the rank of General. His awards, in addition to the Medal of Honor, include the Distinguished Service Medal with Clusters and the Distinguished Flying Cross, the British D.F. C. and a host of other foreign awards.

On July 6, 1989 President George Bush awarded Doolittle the Presidential Medal of Freedom, and on Veterans Day that year he was honored at Oakland, California's North Field with the establishment of a

The legend of the Doolittle raid was enhanced by the Ted Lawson book (he was one of the Tokyo raiders), *ThirtySeconds Over Tokyo*, and further burnished by a an MGM movie. Spencer Tracy played the role of Doolittle. (Credit: Film Favorites

special room and exhibit bearing his name at the Western Aerospace Museum. President George Bush spoke and the 92 year-old Doolittle was present.

Lowell Thomas, Quentin Reynolds and Carroll Glines have all written biographies of Doolittle. With Glines, Doolittle collaborated on a book containing his memoirs in 1991. It is titled, **I Could Never be so Lucky Again.**

He died in 1993 and was buried with full military honors at Arlington Cemetery, Virginia.

KIRK DOUGLAS

Born in Amsterdam, New York in1916 of Jewish-Russian immigrant parents, Douglas worked as a waiter to put himself through St. Lawrence University. He was such a good college wrestler that he wrestled professionally helping to put himself through the New York Academy of Dramatic Arts. He made a Broadway debut in bit roles just before enlisting in the Navy.

He was an enlisted man assigned to an anti-submarine patrol vessel. Serving in the Pacific as an ensign, he was seriously injured because of a premature depth charge explosion and returned to San Diego. After five months hospitalization he was granted a medical discharge in 1944.

In a scene from the movie, *In Harm's Way*, Kirk Douglas clinches with a Hollywood damsel. (Credit: Film Favorites)

Kirk Douglas (center) in deep trouble with the Germans in a scene fIn a scene from the movie, *The Heroes of Telemark*. (Credit: Film Favorites)

He returned to Broadway but soon headed for Hollywood and his first screen appearance in **The Strange Love of Martha Ivers** (1946). With rugged good looks Douglas found steady work in a variety of roles and by 1950 was an established box office star.

He was nominated for Academy Awards for three films: **Champion** (1949), **The Bad And the Beautiful** (1953) and **Lust For Life** (1956). His portrayal of Vincent Van Gogh in **Lust For Life** won the New York Critics Award for Best Actor.

Douglas has appeared in some sixty movies to date, with memorable performances in an array of westerns, dramas, and action adventures. Some of them are: **Young Man With a Horn** (1950), **20,000 Leagues Under the Sea** (1954), **Gunfight at the O.K. Corral** (1957), **Paths of Glory** (1958), **Spartacus** (1960), **Seven Days in May** (1964), **The Fury** (1978) and **The Man From Snowy River** (1982).

He has acted in movies in several foreign countries and formed his own production company several years ago. For his services to the United States as an ambassador of goodwill for the State Department and the U.S. Information Agency he was awarded the Presidential Medal of Freedom in 1981. And in 1988 he received a career achievement award from the National Board of Review. He has also been honored by France and Germany.

DWIGHT EISENHOWER

The 34th President of the United States, Dwight David Eisenhower, was born on October 14, 1890 in Denison, Texas of a farm family. He graduated from the U.S. Military Academy in 1915, commissioned a second lieutenant of infantry, and the following year married Mamie Doud. They had two children, Dwight, who died as a child and John, who became an Army professional like his father.

General Eisenhower climbs in the rear seat of a specially adapted P-51 fighter to get a panoramic view of the Normandy invasion in June 1944. Maj. Gen. Pete Quesada (left) is the pilot. (Credit: Lambert Archives)

General Eisenhower inspects his troops. (Credit: Campbell Archives)

He did not serve in France during World War I. Recognized early in his military career as having administrative and political talents, he spent much of his early career in staff assignments.

With the outbreak of World War II and planning for a second front in North Africa, he was named to command Allied forces for the November 1942 invasion of French Morocco and French Algiers.

His success in that venture and ability to work with Allied leaders caused him to be appointed Commanding General Allied Powers European Theatre of Operations, the man who would lead the invasion of Northern Europe.

After a one and one-half year assembly and training of an invasion army in England, "Ike" had the sole, awesome responsibility of ordering the historic

"Ike" looks grim during the Battle of the Bulge, December 1944. (Campbell Archives)

Gen. Dwight D. Eisenhower's
The *TRUE GLORY*

Distributed by Columbia Pictures · for Office of War Information through War Activities Committee · Motion Picture Indu...

General Eisenhower talks with Army nurses at the front in 1944. The scene is from the documentary, *True Glory*, by Columbia Pictures. (Credit: Film Favorites)

assault. "The Great Crusade", as he termed it - D-Day - commenced on June 6, 1944, when Allied forces breached Hitler's "Fortress Europe" and returned to the Continent to wrest it from three years of Nazi occupation and start the drive to end the war.

After the war he was named Supreme Commander Allied Powers Europe and resigned that title and his Army rank of five star general in July 1952. In the intervening period he was president of Columbia University from 1948-1952. He ran for the presidency of the U.S. on the Republican ticket in 1951. One of his campaign pledges was to end the two year stalemated war in Korea. He won election and kept that promise, going to Korea and helping to engineer an armistice in 1953.

Ike won a second term as president and served until 1962 after which time he went into semi-retirement at Gettysburg where he wrote two books, **Mandate for Change** and **Waging Peace**.

This genuine American hero died on March 29, 1969 and was buried in Abilene, Kansas.

DOUG FAIRBANKS JR.

Born in 1909 the son of Doug Fairbanks, a silent movie star, and mother Anna Beth Sully, "Young Doug," as he was referred to in Hollywood, began his movie career in the 1930s. **Little Caesar** (1931) and **Prisoner of Zenda** (1937) were two of his earliest. He often played the swashbuckler. In 1938 he married actress Joan Crawford.

Famous and popular, Fairbanks was a friend of President Franklin D. Roosevelt and undertook a mission to the principal capitals of South America at FDR's request in 1941. When he returned he sought active duty and was granted a commission as a lieutenant, junior grade in the Naval Reserve and a job with the Navy Department in Washington, DC.

But this didn't suit Fairbanks who requested an assignment in a combat theatre. What he ended up doing was entirely in character with his swashbuckling movie roles.

He first saw convoy duty in the North Atlantic, but because of a friendship with Admiral Lord Louis Mountbatten, Fairbanks got a job with British Commando forces and helped in planning the August 1942 Dieppe raid. A year later he participated in the invasion of Sicily operating with U.S. commando units.

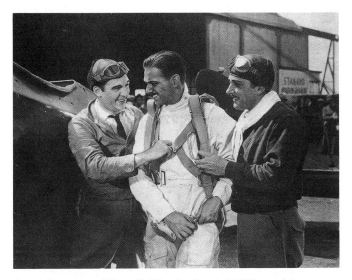

Scene from one of Doug Fairbanks' (center) 1932 movies, *Parachute Jumper*. (Credit: Film Favorites)

Doug Fairbanks (left) as Sinbad the Sailor, a typical swashbuckler role, eyes Maureen O'Hara (Credit: Film Favorites)

Commander Doug Fairbanks Jr. (Credit: The Academy of Motion Picture Arts and Sciences)

When the invasion of Southern France was undertaken, in August 1944, he was given command of a six ship Special Operations Group (two British gunboats and four American PT boats) conducting a commando raid and diversion near Nice. Fairbanks had the satisfaction of hearing Radio Berlin announce that the Nice area had been bombarded by "four or five battleships."

After the war he returned briefly to Hollywood and made only three more movies before moving to London (with his second wife Mary Lee Hartford) to act in British films. An avowed anglophile, Fairbanks also did a London based anthology series for American TV and sometimes acted in British made TV dramas.

He and his wife left London for Palm Beach, Florida where he co-authored three books: **The Fairbanks Album** (1975), **The Salad Days** (1988) and **A Hell of a War** (1993), the latter about his personal experiences in World War II.

His wife died in 1988 and Fairbanks continues to reside in Florida.

BOB FELLER

One of the great fast ball pitchers of all time was born in 1918 in Van Meter, Iowa. He joined the Cleveland Indians of the American League in 1936 and soon became a standout pitcher. He earned the nick name, "Rapid Robert".

He left baseball in 1942 to join the U.S. Navy and did his share of PR for the government but spent considerable time in Pacific combat zones before receiving his honorable discharge in 1945. He had attained the rank of Chief Petty Officer.

Returning to the Indians before the end of the 1945 season, he continued to pitch for them until his retirement after the end of the 1956 season. During sixteen seasons in the majors he had a lifetime ERA of 3.25 and won 266 games, appearing in just one world series.

He was elected to the Baseball Hall of Fame in 1962.

Chief Petty Officer Bob Feller during his WW II stint in the Navy. (Credit: National Baseball Library Cooperstown, NY)

HENRY FONDA

Born May 16, 1905 in Grand Isle, Nebraska, Fonda's family moved to Omaha when he was six. He enrolled in the University of Minnesota seeking to be a journalist but dropped out after two years and took an office job in Omaha. In 1925 he played a stage role at the Omaha Community Playhouse and thus began a distinguished acting career that spanned over five decades.

Fonda did summer stock then played Broadway and went on to Hollywood and the movies in 1934. With his good looks and natural style he became a box office favorite with movies like **The Farmer Takes a Wife** (1935), **The Trail of the Lonesome Pine** (1936), **Jesse James** and **Drums Along the Mohawk** (1939), and **The Grapes of Wrath** (1940).

He interrupted his movie career in 1942 to enlist in the U.S. Navy. Fonda received a commission after an OCS course and was slated for film making. However, he talked his way out of that assignment and into sea duty and served in the Pacific as an assistant operations and intelligence officer aboard the seaplane tender *Curtiss* . He also served as a courier to the staff of Admiral Chester Nimitz. Lieutenant Fonda was awarded the Bronze Star and Presidential Unit Citation.

In a book by his biographer, Howard Teichmann, Fonda relates how he dragged a parachute bag of liquor from the States all the way to Kwajalein Island to use for bartering. Leaving the bag temporarily in an airfield office, he delivered dispatches to Admiral Nimitz then aboard an aircraft carrier at anchor in the

Henry Fonda (center) recreates his award winning stage role of Mr. Roberts for the Warner Bros. movie. Supporting roles were played by William Powell (left) as Doc and Jack Lemmon (right) as Ensign Pulver. (Credit: Film Favorites)

Henry Fonda (left) reports to superiors played by Robert Ryan (center) and Dana Andrews in a scene from the Warners Bros. movie *Battle of the Bulge*. (Credit: Film Favorites)

lagoon. When he returned Fonda discovered that his precious bag had been loaded on board a transport plane, then tossed off to the steel landing mat below and returned to the spot he had left it. After an 8,000 mile journey his bourbon was leaking all over Kwajalein and through his spare clothing.

Fonda returned to his movie career to partake in several classic John Ford epics: **My Darling Clementine, The Fugitive** and **Fort Apache.** In 1948 he returned to the Broadway stage for the title role in **Mister Roberts.** The play lasted three years to rave reviews, then was done for the screen in 1955 with Fonda again in the starring role.

Alternating between stage and screen for several years Fonda was acclaimed for roles in **The Caine Mutiny Court Martial** (Broadway, 1955), **War and Peace** (1956), **Advise and Consent** (1962), **Fail Safe** (1964), **The Rounders** and **In Harm's Way** (1965).

He ventured successfully into TV series and specials, his portrayal of **Clarence Darrow** being critically acclaimed.

Fonda continued making movies until 1981 when he was given an honorary Academy Award for a lifetime of achievement. His last film was **On Golden Pond** and for that performance he won an Oscar. He died in 1982.

Fonda (left) plays the part of Admiral Chester Nimitz in the movie *Battle of Midway.* Glenn Ford (center) portrayed Adm. Ray Spruance and Robert Mitchum is Adm. Bull Halsey. (Credit: Film Favorites)

GERALD FORD

Born Gerald R. Ford, Jr. on July 14, 1913 in Omaha, Nebraska, his family moved to Grand Rapids Michigan where Ford was the captain of his high school football team. He received an athletic scholarship to the University of Michigan were he starred as a varsity center. Graduating in 1935 he accepted a job as assistant coach at Yale which enabled him to pursue his law degree. He graduated in the top third of his class in 1941, returned to Michigan and passed the bar.

He volunteered for military service and was accepted as an ensign in the Naval Reserve in April 1942. After failing flight school he was assigned to the aircraft carrier *Monterey* as assistant navigator. He served through the First Battle of the Philippine Sea,

Lt. Comdr. Gerald R. Ford. (Credit: President Ford Library)

the Philippine invasion and the campaigns to the shores of Japan, receiving his honorable discharge from active duty in 1946. He continued in the Naval Reserve until 1963.

In 1948 he married Elizabeth (Betty) Bloomer.

Ford ran for Congress and was elected in 1949. He served in that body until 1973, (as minority leader from 1965) when he was appointed vice president of the United States under Nixon. On the resignation of President Nixon he became the 38th President of the United States and served until defeated in the election of 1977.

Gerry Ford (left) on the flight deck of aircraft carrier *Monterey*, the South Pacific 1943. (Credit: President Ford Library)

He is presently retired and living in Scottsdale, Arizona with his wife Betty.

GLENN FORD

Young Glenn Ford in *Flight Lieutenant*. (Credit: Film Favorites)

Movie star Glenn Ford was born in Quebec, Canada but grew up in Santa Monica, California where he attended high school. He made his film debut in 1939 in **Heaven With a Barbed Wire Fence**.

He made the movie **Flight Lieutenant** in 1942 shortly before enlisting in the Marine Corps. He rose from the ranks to become an officer and was in charge of a camera crew during the Normandy, D-Day invasion. Near the end of World War II his film crew recorded the horrible conditions at the German Concentration Camp of Dachau, in Poland.

Ford returned to a highly active life in motion pictures and was leading man to movie sirens such as Rita Hayworth in movies like **Gilda**. He played in many westerns and also made several memorable war movies, **Gallant Journey** in 1946, **Is Paris Burning** in 1966 and **The Battle of Midway** in 1976.

Glenn Ford seems oblivious to Rita Hayworth's display of leg in this scene from the movie, *Gilda*. (Credit: Film Favorites)

Glenn Ford (center) and Ernest Borgnine (right) in a scene from the submarine movie, *Torpedo Run.* (Credit: Film Favorites)

During the Vietnam war he returned to the Marines and served in the field, finally retiring with the rank of colonel. Ford recalled with pride that during the heat of battle in Vietnam a soldier said, "You're just like us, you're one of us."

In a scene from the movie, *Is Paris Burning*, Glenn Ford (right) and Robert Stack. (Credit: Film Favorites)

JOE FOSS

One of America's most recognizable and enduring heroes of World War II, Joe Foss was born on April 17, 1915 in Sioux Falls, South Dakota, son of a farm family.

Joe's father, Frank, was intrigued with the romance of flight and talked for years about buying an airplane. He took the family to see Charles Lindbergh and the "Spirit of St. Louis" when they dropped into Sioux Falls in 1927. In 1933 son and father flew for the first time, buying a pair of 75 cent tickets for seats on a Ford Tri-motor and a half-hour over Southeast Dakota. Frank Foss was accidentally killed a few months later when he stepped on a downed power line. It was Joe's senior year in high school and he remained imbued with his father's dream of flight. After receiving a B.S. at the University of South Dakota in 1940, he joined the Marine Corps.

Foss completed flight training and with war then raging in the Pacific he wanted to go into fighters, but the Marine Corps deemed the 27 year-old too old for fighters and kept side tracking him into other types of aircraft. Finally he found a home as Executive Officer (second in command) of VMF-121 and arrived on Guadalcanal in the Solomon Islands in October 1942. Guadalcanal had been invaded the previous month and the Japanese were still battling ferociously to hang on. Air and sea battles swirled around the island and the issue was in doubt.

Flying Grumman F4F Wildcats Captain Foss destroyed 26 enemy planes in aerial combat in just three months. His squadron was relieved and Joe went home to a hero's welcome. He received the Medal of Honor and Distinguished Flying Cross and was seen by thousands of Americans at war bond rallies. His rugged good looks became familiar because of heavy press coverage. The South Dakotan had not just achieved a Horatio Alger dream, he had become the highest scoring ace in World War II (to that point) and had equaled the World War I record of 26 victories scored by Capt. Eddie Rickenbacker.

Late in the war Foss returned to the Pacific with his own squadron, VMF-115. Flying F4U Corsairs from Bougainville, they bombed and strafed Japanese bases in the Solomon Islands, but these bases had been bypassed and no enemy aircraft remained for aerial defense.

In the postwar era Foss transferred to the independent U.S. Air Force and formed the South Dakota contingent of the Air National Guard. He led an acrobatic unit of P-51 Mustangs from the South Dakota Air Guard on a 1950s tour of air shows. His unit was recalled during the Korean War but without Foss, as the Air Force had a rule that Medal of Honor winners could not return to combat.

Jumping into politics with his usual brand of enthusiasm, he was elected to the South Dakota legislature in 1948-1953. In 1954 he was elected Republican Governor of South Dakota and held the office until 1958.

Capt. Joe Foss, and cigar, stands by his Grumman Wildcat on Guadalcanal, Solomon Islands, 1942. (Credit: US Navy)

Some of the pilots of VMF-121 pose on Guadalcanal. Foss sits astride the fuselage, cap brim turned up. (Credit: USMC)

Out of politics Foss stayed in the public eye as he participated in many civic groups: the President's Council on Fitness and Sports, the White House Conference on Handicapped Individuals and the Endowment for Community Leadership (a fund to help homeless). He also found time to be on the Air Force Academy Board of Directors and the Board of the National Rifle Association. He was President of the NRA 1988-90.

Living now in Scottsdale, Arizona with Donna, his wife of fifty some years, he continues to lecture widely, and continues to receive honors and awards.

Capt. Joe Foss visits the Grumman Aircraft Corp. plant to thank them for the workmanship on the F4F Wildcat that he flew on Guadalcanal. (Credit: Lambert Archives)

Brig. Gen. Joe Foss, postwar commander of the South Dakota Air National Guard. (Credit: South Dakota Historical Society)

CLARK GABLE

Lt. Clark Gable at gunnery practice with belts of .50 caliber machine gun bullets slung over his shoulders. (Credit: Maxwell AFB Archives)

One of Hollywood's most handsome stars was born in Cadiz, Ohio on February 1, 1901. As a teenager he had an urge for the stage, but the reality of earning a living kept him at odd jobs - oil well "monkey", lumberjack, salesman - until he landed in Hollywood at age 23.

He got a bit part in his first movie in 1924 but without great success or starring roles. Heading to Broadway, he struggled on the stage for several years, but a traveling show took him back west. Lionel Barrymore befriended him and tried to help with various studio introductions. But none would accept him, the mogul Darryl F. Zanuck dismissed him with the now famous quote, "His ears are too big." Finally he got a villains role in a William Boyd western and MGM signed him to a contract.

Gable, who had appeared in just seven movies between 1924-1927, was in no less than thirteen in 1931, and with some fine starring roles he gained sudden popularity with movie fans. He had a steady run of work in many successful movies through the 1930s and by the end of that decade he was dubbed "The King of Hollywood." He won an Academy Award for **It Happened One Night** (1934), then in 1939 he appeared in the starring roll of Hollywood's all time box office hit, **Gone With The Wind.**

The enormous success that Gable had achieved on the screen failed to translate into his personal life. He had two failed marriages when, in 1939, he met and married actress Carole Lombard, the female sex symbol of her day. The union seemed ideal and Gable seemed to have everything until January 1942 when Carole was killed in an airplane crash. Deeply despondent, Gable joined the Army Air Force and completed Officer Candidate School. He was over forty years of age, unsuited for many military tasks, and military authorities were reluctant to place the renowned man in any sort of jeopardy. He could easily have worked on stateside film documentaries. But he pressed for foreign service and became a combat photographer with the Eighth Air Force in England.

Gable flew many missions over Europe as a crew member in heavy bombers, shooting not only his camera, but manning defensive guns. He gained the respect of his fellow airmen and won the Distinguished Flying Cross and Air Medal for his courageous service. He returned in 1945 with the rank of major.

Capt. Clark Gable leans from the waist gun turret of a B-17 bomber prior to a mission from England. (Credit: USAF)

He returned to Hollywood but appeared in movies sparingly, making only 22 more between 1945 and 1961. He had a bout with alcoholism, two more marriages and health problems. With his last wife, Kay Spreckels, he had a son he never got to see. Gable died of a heart attack just after a stellar performance opposite Marilyn Monroe in the 1961 hit, **The Misfits.**

A listing of his best movies is difficult since he had so many fine performances, but here are a few from the postwar era: **The Hucksters** (1947), **Command Decision** (1948), **Across the Wide Missouri** (1951), **Mogambo** (1953), **The Tall Men** (1955), **Band of Angels** (1957), **Run Silent, Run Deep** (1958), **But Not For Me** (1959) and **The Misfits** (1961).

Capt. Clark Gable poses with one of the B-17 Flying Fortress bombers that he rode over Germany, it must have reminded him of Rhett Butler. (Credit: Ted Nevill via Campbell Archives)

Clark Gable (right) plays a role he was well suited for based on his WW II combat experience. The movie was MGMs *Command Decision.* John Hodiak is on the left. (Credit: Film Favorites)

JOHN GLENN

America's first man to orbit the earth was born John H. Glenn, Jr. on July 18, 1921 in Cambridge, Ohio. He was attending Muskingum College when World War II broke out.

He entered the Naval aviation cadet program and upon graduation received his wings and a commission in the U.S. Marine Corps in 1943. He was assigned to the Marshall Islands, joining VMF-155, and flew 59 combat missions in F4U Corsair fighters.

Following World War II he had duty in China and Guam, then returned to Corpus Christi, Texas as an instructor. He later attended the Amphibious Warfare Training Center at Quantico, Virginia.

During the Korean war he flew sixty-three missions with VMF-311 in F9F Panther jets, and then as an exchange pilot flew 27 more missions in the F-86 Saberjet with the 25th Fighter Squadron, USAF. He downed three Mig-15 jet fighters in aerial combat. Colonel Glenn has been awarded the Distinguished

Flying Cross with four Oak Leaf Clusters and the Air Medal with eighteen Clusters for his combat exploits.

In 1952 he attended Test Pilot School at the Naval Air Test Center, Patuxent River, Maryland and after graduation was project officer on a number of aircraft. He was assigned to the Fighter Design Branch of the Navy in Washington from 1956 to 1959 during which period he attended the University of Maryland. In 1957 he was the first to maintain supersonic speed throughout a transcontinental flight.

It was in 1959 that he was selected as one of the seven original Project Mercury astronauts, and on February 20, 1962 he rode the Mercury Capsule, "Friendship 7", into space, the first American to engage in an orbital mission. After three orbits of the earth, reaching a maximum altitude of 162 statute miles, he brought his capsule back to a parachute splash down in the Atlantic.

Glenn left NASA in 1964 and retired from the Marine Corps on January 1, 1965. At that time he

John Glenn's Korean war mount, an F-86 named "Mig Mad Marine". The three stars just below the cockpit windscreen represent air combat victories. (Credit: Campbell Archives)

Senator John Glenn (Credit: Senator Glenn's office)

HANK GREENBERG

He was born in New York City in 1911 as Henry B. Greenberg but was known to a generation of baseball fans as "Hammerin' Hank".

In 1930 he joined the Detroit Tigers of the American League playing outfield and first base for them for 15 years.

He joined the Army Air Force in 1941, went through officer candidate school and received a commission as second lieutenant. He worked in a variety of special services and administrative roles and was honorably discharged as a Captain in 1945.

Returning to the Tigers, he continued to be a stellar long ball hitter until his retirement after the 1947 season. He was traded briefly at the end of the 1947 season to Pittsburgh in the National League. During a lifetime he had a batting average of .313 and hit 331 homeruns. He played in four world series and was inducted into the Baseball Hall of Fame in 1956.

It is generally conceded that Hank broke the unstated barrier to Jews that had existed for decades in baseball's major leagues. He died in 1986.

Senator John Glenn. (Credit: Senator Glenn's office)

entered business as an executive and director with Royal Crown Cola Co. and continued in that capacity until he ran for the Senate of the United States from his native Ohio in 1974. He was elected to the Senate as a Democrat and continues in that office to this writing.

In additions to his many United States military decorations he has been awarded the Congressional Space Medal of Honor (1978) the Centennial Award of the National Geographic Society (1988) and honorary degrees from Muskingum College and Nihon University, Tokyo.

Senator Glenn has written **We Seven** (co-author) and **P.S. I Listened to Your Heart Beat.**

Capt Hank Greenberg during his WW II stint in the Army Air Force. (Credit: National Baseball Museum, Cooperstown, NY)

BULL HALSEY

The man who would be known as "Bull" was born William F. Halsey in Elizabeth, New Jersey in 1882. He graduated from the United States Naval Academy in 1904.

He was a Rear Admiral by 1938 and on December 7, 1941 commanded a Task Force that was a few hundred miles off Oahu when the Japanese struck. Bull was a tenacious fighter and advocate of carrier warfare. He led one or another of the Pacific fleets in virtually every major engagement of the war except Midway, when he was sidelined in a hospital. He achieved Admiral rank on December 11, 1945 as he headed the Third Fleet.

Shortly after the Japanese capitulation Halsey led the Navy into Tokyo Bay and dropped anchor. Knowing that there were American prisoners of war in a camp on the edge of the Bay he summoned members of his staff told them to take his admirals gig and ferry the captives back to the fleet. "Our boys are over there," he said. "Go get them."

His decorations include the Navy Cross, Distinguished Service Medal with three clusters, Distinguished Service Medal (Army), and a host of foreign awards.

United Artists did a movie depicting the life of Admiral Halsey with Jimmy Cagney in the lead role. Titled **The Gallant Hours**, it was produced and directed by Robert Montgomery.

Halsey retired on April 1, 1947 and died in 1959.

Adm. William F. Halsey (right) chats with his boss, Adm. Chester Nimitz. (Credit: Admiral Nimitz Museum)

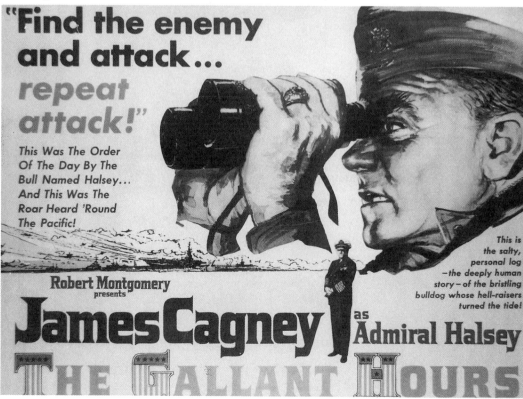

Movie poster for Halsey's film biography. (Credit: Film Favorites)

TOM HARMON

Born Thomas D. Harmon on September 28, 1919, in Gary, Indiana, the son of a policeman, he performed gridiron exploits that made him a national figure.

He attended the University of Michigan playing varsity football in 1938, 39 and 40. He was a blocking back as a sophomore, then was shifted to left half in 1939. He was all-American in 1939 and 1940 and won the Heisman Trophy, Maxwell Trophy and the Washington Touchdown Trophy for his performance in 1940. He was also named the Big Ten's Most Valuable Player his last year.

On graduation he became a sports broadcaster and director of sports for radio station WJR in Detroit.

In November 1941, with America just one month away from war, he enlisted in the Army Aviation Cadet program. After winning his wings and commission he was assigned to a bomber unit, and in the process of ferrying the aircraft to a war zone he crashed but survived. He was later sent to the China-Burma-India Theatre of Operations and joined the 449th Fighter Squadron of the 51st Fighter Group, flying the

Tom Harmon (Credit: U. of Michigan)

Tom Harmon, "Old 98" to the University of Michigan faithful, running around end. (Credit: U. of Michigan)

Lockheed P-38. He was shot down, and managed to evade capture and escape with the help of Chinese guerrillas. He was lost for 30 days during the ordeal and reported "Missing in Action."

He was awarded the Silver Star and Purple Heart.

After leaving military service he went to Los Angeles where he had two years of pro football with the Los Angeles Rams. Subsequently he worked in radio and TV as a sports director and broadcaster. He married film actress Elyse Knox and they had three children.

MARK O. HATFIELD

Born in Dallas, Oregon on July 22, 1922, his father was a railroad worker and his mother a teacher. When only ten years old Mark was introduced to Republican politics by his mother as he helped her deliver campaign literature. He enrolled at Willamette University and received his B.A. there in 1943.

Credit: Senator Mark O. Hatfield's office

Immediatley after college graduation he enlisted in the U.S. Navy and attended officer candidate school. On graduation and receipt of his ensign's commission he was assigned to the Pacific Fleet. He was stationed on a landing craft and participated in the invasions of Iwo Jima and Okinawa. At the surrender of the Japanese he was one of the first Americans to land in Hiroshima and witness the effects of the atom bomb on that city. After that he was dispatched to transport Chinese Nationalist troops from French Indo-China to Formosa. Completing 31 months of service, he returned to the States and an honorable discharge with the rank of lieutenant (junior grade).

He enrolled at Willamette University again to study law, but switched to Stanford and the pursuit of an M.A. in political science. On achieving graduation he returned to Willamette to teach political science. In 1950 he became involved in Republican politics and won a seat in the Oregon legislature. He served as a state representative until 1954 and then in the senate from 1954 to 1956.

Hatfield won the governorship in 1956, the youngest in the history of Oregon. While in that office he became prominent in national Republican circles supporting the civil rights cause and forthrightly opposing the expansion of the Vietnamese conflict. He won a seat in the U.S. Senate in 1966 and has been in that post ever since.

The senator is currently Chairman of the Appropriations Committee.

STERLING HAYDEN

Born Sterling Relyea Walter on March 26, 1917 in Montclair, New Jersey, he was a school dropout with a longing for the sea. He worked on ships until able to buy his own schooner at age 22. He helped fund the purchase by modeling.

In 1940 his tall, blond good looks won him a movie contract and the studio featured him in **Virginia** followed by **Bahama Passage.**

With war on the horizon the restless Hayden joined the Marine Corps, went through officer candidate school and was commissioned. During parachute training he was injured and after recovery worked with the OSS in commando-like operations in the Adriatic Sea, running supplies to Yugoslav guerrillas. He was honorably discharged as a captain in 1945. During the war he was married to Madeleine Carroll, one of Hollywood's leading ladies, a union that lasted for only four years.

During his Yugoslavian service he became associated with the Communists and joined the Communist Party in 1946 but terminated that membership in six months after thinking better of the matter. This brief association, however, caused him to be questioned by a House of Representatives Committee on Un-American Activities in 1951, along with several other Hollywood figures. Since he had voluntarily gone before the Committee to admit his youthful indiscretion, he was not blacklisted as were many of his colleagues.

He worked in films only spasmodically, his free spirit causing him to periodically sail the seas. He had another marriage that failed although he had four children by his second wife. In 1959 he took all four on a cruise to the South Pacific aboard his ship *Wanderer* despite a court order forbidding the journey.

Sterling Hayden in a World War II war movie, *Flat Top*. (Credit: Film Favorites)

Sterling Hayden in a scene from the movie, *The Eternal Sea*. (Credit: Film Favorites)

He did movies between adventures as the spirit moved him. Some were exceptional and some mediocre. He is best remembered for his work in: **Blaze of Noon** (1947), **The Asphalt Jungle** (1950), **The Killing** (1956), **Dr. Strangelove** (1964) and **The Godfather** (1972).

He wrote his autobiography, **The Wanderer** in 1963, and published a novel of the sea, **Voyage**, in 1976. In 1983 he was the subject of a documentary film, **Lighthouse of Chaos**. He died of prostate cancer in 1986.

PETER LIND HAYES

Born in 1925 in San Francisco, California. His father died when he was just two and his mother, a vaudeville performer moved to New Rochelle, New York. Peter toured with his mother summers and appeared in one of her stage skits as early as nine. He worked the vaudeville circuit for two years.

With the advent of talking movies and the death of vaudeville the family moved to California and young Peter made his film debut in 1940. In the next couple of years he appeared in some fifteen movies, usually in a supporting role, while working the stage of his mother's nightclub as a comedian.

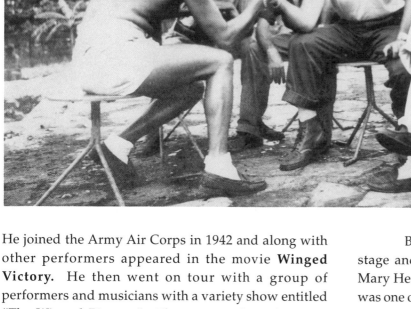

Peter Lind Hayes arm wrestling in the Pacific. (Credit: Peter Lind Hayes)

He joined the Army Air Corps in 1942 and along with other performers appeared in the movie **Winged Victory.** He then went on tour with a group of performers and musicians with a variety show entitled "The Winged Pigeons". They put on their show 620 times in the Pacific, where Hayes earned a Bronze Star and rose to the rank of technical sergeant. He received his honorable discharge in December 1945.

Peter Lind Hayes, during his TV days, by Norman Rockwell. (Credit: Peter Lind Hayes)

Back at work, Hayes alternated between the stage and night clubs usually teamed with his wife, Mary Healy, an accomplished actress. That same team was one of the early entries in television with CBS series, "The Star of the Family." They were retained by Arthur Godfrey as permanent substitutes for his show in 1953. For several years they worked radio, TV, movies and the stage alternately until concentrating on the television talk and variety format, "The Peter Lind Hayes Show" in 1959.

VAN HEFLIN

Born in Walters, Oklahoma in 1910 as Emmett Evan Heflin, Jr., he was educated at the University of Oklahoma and also attended the Yale School of Drama.

He first tried the stage and got his Broadway break in 1928. This brought him to the attention of Hollywood and he made his film debut in the 1936 movie, **A Woman Rebels.** He won an Academy Award for his 1942 performance in **Johnny Eager.**

In 1942 he enlisted in the U.S. Army and after attending officer candidate school and winning a commission, he served as an artillery officer. He was honorably discharged in 1945.

Van Heflin in the movie, *Battle Cry*. (Credit: Film Favorites)

Returning to Hollywood after the war he gave many fine performances in complex dramatic roles. Some of his best are: **The Strange Love of Martha Ivers** (1964), **Madame Bovary** (1949), **Shane** (1953), **The Raid** (1954), **Battle Cry** (1955), **Patterns** (1956), **3:10 to Yuma** (1957), **They Came to Cordura** (1959), **The Greatest Story Ever Told** (1965) and **Airport** (1970).

Heflin also won critical acclaim for his Broadway efforts in "A View From the Bridge" and "A Case of Libel". He died of a heart attack in 1971.

CHARLTON HESTON

Born in 1923 in Evanston, Illinois, as Charles Carter, few actors have appeared in more epic sagas. He attended his hometown college, Northwestern University, in speech and drama studies, and it was there that he first appeared on stage.

He enlisted in the U.S. Army Air Force in 1942 and after a period of training was assigned to the 77th Bomb Squadron of the Eleventh Air Force in Alaska as a gunner on a North American B-25 Mitchell.

Returning after World War II he made his stage debut in stock productions, then made his Broadway debut in "Anthony and Cleopatra" in 1947. He was an early entrant into television, starring in dramas, where film makers noticed his rugged good looks. His Hollywood premier was in 1949 and from that time on he was a fixture on the screen for 50 years.

Charlton Heston in a scene from Universal's *Gray Lady Down*. (Credit: Film Favorites)

He won an Academy Award as Best Actor for the 1959 movie, **Ben Hur**, and has made over 60 films. Some of his most memorable are: **The Naked Jungle** (1954), **The Far Horizons** (1955), **The Ten Commandments** (1956), **The Big Country** (1958), **El Cid** (1961), **55 Days at Peking** (1963), **The Greatest Story Ever Told** and **The Agony and the Ecstasy** (1965), **Planet of the Apes** (1968), **The Hawaiians** (1970), **Soylent Green** (1973), **The Three Musketeers** (1975), **Airport** (1975), **Midway** (1976), **Gray Lady Down** (1978), **The Awakening** (1980) and **Tombstone** (1993).

Heston has also taken a try at directing and has been active in the Screen Actors Guild and Republican politics. He was honored with the Gene Hersholt Humanitarian Award at the 1977 Academy Awards.

WILLIAM HOLDEN

Born in 1918 in O'Fallon, Illinois, as William Franklin Beedle, Jr., he was a member of a family that was well off, his father being a corporate executive. Early in his life he moved to Southern California and attended South Pasadena High and Pasadena Junior College. It was in college that he began working with a theatric group and was spotted by a talent scout.

His first small movie part was in 1938, followed by minor roles in 1939, until he got the lead in **Golden Boy** (1939) and became a star. Holden was in a dozen movies before he left for the service in World War II.

He enlisted in the U.S. Army in 1942 and, after attending officer candidate school, he won a commission and was assigned to a Special Service unit responsible for entertainment.

Early in 1944 Holden received the news that his younger brother, Robert a Navy fighter pilot serving with VF-18 off the aircraft carrier *Bunker Hill* , had been killed in action. William Holden served in his post until discharged in 1945 as a Captain.

Returning to the film world he was first cast in "Mr. Clean Cut" situations, but his versatility and depth eventually put him in every conceivable type of film role. He received an Oscar as Best Actor in the 1953 **Stalag 17**. Some of his other memorable roles were in the following films: **Blaze of Noon** (1947), **The Dark Past** (1949), **Sunset Boulevard** (1950), **Executive Suite**

William Holden (center) in the Paramount movie, *Submarine Command.* Bill Bendix is left and Don Taylor at right. (Credit: Film Favorites)

Bill Holden extricates himself from a downed jet fighter in James Michener's Korean war movie, *The Bridges at Toko-Ri.* (Credit: Film Favorites)

(1954), **The Bridges at Toko-Ri** (1955), **Picnic** (1956), **The Bridge on the River Kwai** (1957), **The Horse Soldiers** (1959), **Alvarez Kelly** (1966), **The Devil's Brigade** (1968), **The Wild Bunch** (1969), **Network** (1976) and **S.O.B.** (1981), his last film.

Holden died in 1981.

William Holden (center) is bracket by stars Alec Quiness (left) and Jack Hawkins in a publicity still for the 1957 epic war movie, *Bridge on the River Kwai.* (Credit: Film Favorites)

BOB HOPE

America's most enduring comedian for the better part of this century was born in England as Leslie Townes Hope in 1903. In 1934 he married Delores Reade.

He came to America as a young man and spent many years in vaudeville and musical comedy before establishing himself as a star in Hollywood films. His movies, all light hearted, include: **The Big Broadcast** and, **Thanks For the Memory** (1938), **The Road to**

Bob Hope and Frances Langford mount a P-47 Thunderbolt fighter of the 78th Fighter Group at Duxford, England in 1943. (Credit: Campbell Archives)

Morocco (1942), **The Paleface** (1948), **The Great Lover** (1949), **The Seven Little Foys** (1954), **Call Me Bwana** (1963), and **How to Commit Marriage** (1969).

Hope's comedic talents lent themselves well to radio, and with the advent of TV he was a regular on many variety shows.

Bob Hope was not a member of the armed forces in World War II, but no entertainer gave more of himself to the war effort. He constantly organized USO troops and appeared with them throughout Europe, North Africa and the Pacific. Thousands of GI scrap books dating from World War II show candid shots of Hope and some of his troop doing musical and comedy shows in far off places. Nor did his efforts end with World War II. Under the auspices of the USO Hope brought live entertainment shows to U.S. forces abroad during and between the wars in Korea, Viet Nam and up to and including Desert Storm. Many of these shows were performed over the Christmas holidays.

For his selfless service Bob Hope has been awarded the Congressional Gold Medal by President Kennedy, the Medal of Freedom by President Johnson, the People to People Award by President Eisenhower

Bob Hope felt right at home in England in 1943. (Credit: Hope Enterprises)

Some of the regulars who toured Europe and the Pacific with Bob Hope. Left to right: Tony Romano, Patty Thomas, Jerry Colonna, Frances Langford, Bob Hope and Barney Dean. (Credit: Hope Enterprises)

and service medals from all branches of the military. Great Britain has made him Honorary Commander, Order of the British Empire.

His show business awards are also voluminous: Four special Academy Awards, one Emmy, three Peoples Choice Awards for best male entertainer 75-76, The Jean Hersholdt Humanitarian Award and the Criss Award.

Over 90 years of age, Hope has limited his acting, but is still active and living in California with Delores, his wife of 60 years.

Bob Hope in one of his postwar movie roles, *The PrivateNavy of Sergeant O'Farrell.* (Credit: Film Favorites)

Bob Hope on one of his many post war tours of distant overseas bases. (Credit Film Favorites)

RALPH HOUK

Born in Lawrence, Kansas in 1919, as a farm boy, he first played baseball in high school where he was All-State. He began playing his first semi-pro ball with his uncle Charlie's team, the Belvoirs. Signed by Yankee scouts in 1939 he played two years of minor league ball before joining the Army.

Houk became an officer and was shipped to Europe with the 9th Armored Division in World War II. He served with Patton's 3rd Army in the campaign across France then in December 1944 he was involved in the Battle of the Bulge. He took a bullet through the helmet but was not seriously wounded. He served in Europe until the end of the war and was awarded the Silver Star, Bronze Star and Purple Heart. He left the Army in the rank of Major in 1946.

He married Bette Porter in 1948 and they have three children.

Returning to the minor leagues he played three more years then was called up by the New York Yankees, as a reserve catcher from 1950 to 1954. He played in 91 games with a .272 lifetime batting average and appearances in two world series.

The Yankee organization, impressed with Houk's leadership and baseball knowledge, sent him to a managing job with Denver in the minor leagues, and his success there earned him a coaching job with the parent club. He developed the nick name, "Major" in baseball.

His greatest success was as manager of the Yankees for the periods 61-63, 66-73. In 1974 he signed a contract to manage the Detroit Tigers and stayed with that club until 1978. Retiring for a period, he returned to a managers job with the Boston Red Sox from 1981-84. His composite record as a manager shows a .514 winning percentage. His clubs had three first place finishes and won two World Series.

After a final stint in the front office with the Minnesota Twins, he retired to Winter Haven, Florida to golf and fish.

Ralph Houk during his playing days with the New York Yankees. (Credit: National Baseball Library, Cooperstown, NY)

ROCK HUDSON

Born Roy Harold Scherer, Jr., in Winnetka, Illinois on November 17, 1925, Hudson tried out for roles in school plays, but failed to win any because of his inability to remember lines. After high school he worked briefly as a mail carrier then enlisted in the Navy.

He was trained as an aircraft mechanic by the Navy and stationed at an airbase on the island of Samar in the Philippines. After the war, he was granted an honorable discharge in 1946.

Returning to menial jobs in civilian life he still dreamed of acting and found an agent who thought his rugged good looks and six foot-four inch frame were marketable. With a name change (that is pure Hollywood), some dental work, and acting lessons he finally broke into films in 1948. It is rumored that there were multiple takes of his first shot, as he still had trouble remembering his lines.

Clearly his persistence paid off as he became one of Hollywood's leading male stars and a top box office draw through the 1950s, 60, and 70s. He was nominated for an Oscar for **Giant** (1956), and won the Look Magazine Star of the Year award in 1958.

The man who saw so little real combat during his own military service acted in a number of popular war movies. He was also amazingly adept at comedy with a number of bedroom farces opposite Doris Day and a TV series "McMillan and Wife" that ran from 1971-1977. He played a periodic role in the popular prime time soap opera, "Dynasty" (1984-85).

Some of his 60 odd movie hits were: **Bend of the River** (1952), **Magnificent Obsession** (1954), **Battle Hymn** and **A Farewell to Arms** (1957), **Pillow Talk** (1959), **Tobruk** (1967), **The Undefeated** (1969) and **The Ambassador** (1984).

He died in 1985 at age 59 of AIDS, having openly admitted his homosexuality shortly before, the first of the Hollywood stars to go public with the issue.

Rock Hudson (center) and George Peppard (right) in a scene from the movie, *Tobruk*. (Credit: Film Favorites)

60

DAN INOUYE

Born in Honolulu on September 7, 1924, of parents of Japanese ancestry, Daniel K. Inouye became the epitome of the Horatio Alger story of a poor boy rising to great honors despite enormous obstacles.

Young Dan attended Honolulu's McKinley High School, then nicknamed "Tokyo High" for its predominantly Japanese-American enrollment. He earned pocket money by parking cars at Honolulu Stadium and by giving harcuts to fellow students.

When the Japanese raided Oahu on December 7, 1941 Inouye applied his medical aid training to assist with the thousands of wounded. He was part of a first-aid litter team and didn't get home for a week. "We saw a lot of blood, " he recalled of the stunning event. Because of concerns over their loyalty, Americans of Japanese ancestry were initially discharged from the Hawaiian National Guard and rejected by the Selective Service System. For mainland Japanese-Americans it was even worse. They were forced into concentration camps, their property confiscated. All of this occurred despite the fact that there was never one case of sabotage by a Japanese-American.

In June 1942 the government policy toward this American minority changed when the Army announced plans to accept a limited number of Americans of Japanese descent to form a regimental sized infantry unit. Inouye, then an 18 year-old pre-med student at the University of Hawaii, enlisted, trained at Camp Shelby, Mississippi and went to Italy with the 442nd Regimental Combat Team, the "Niesi" (second generation) unit.

Sergeant Inouye spent three months of hard combat in the Rome-Arno Campaign with the U.S. Fifth Army during 1944. Early on he established himself as an outstanding leader with the "Go For Broke" regiment, the Pidgin-English phrase used as a rallying cry on the battlefield. After the invasion of Southern France, August 1944, part of the 442nd was shifted to the Voges Mountain region and spent two of the bloodiest weeks of the war rescuing a Texas battalion surrounded by German forces. Casualties were heavy and Inouye, in the thick of the fighting, won a Bronze Star and a battlefield commission as second lieutenant.

Candid shots of Dan Inouye as a young soldier. (Credit: Senator Inouye's office)

Senator Daniel Inouye. (Credit: Senator Inouye's office)

Returning to Italy as a platoon leader, Inouye led an attack on strong German positions and was shot but continued to advance alone against a machine gun nest. He threw two grenades before his right arm was shattered by a German rifle grenade. Undaunted Inouye threw his last grenade with his left hand and attacked with his submachine gun until downed by a third wound, a bullet in the leg. For this action he won the Distinguished Service Cross (second only to the Medal of Honor) and the Purple Heart with one Oak Leaf Cluster.

He spent 20 months in Army hospitals because of his wounds, but lost his right arm. A member of the most decorated regiment in the U.S. Army, Captain Dan Inouye was one of its most decorated members. The loss of the right arm shattered his dream of a medical career, but undaunted he used his GI Bill to attain a law degree. Along the way he married Margaret Awamura.

After a short term in the Honolulu legislature, Inouye won a seat to the House of Representatives and ran for and won election to the Senate in 1963. He has chaired many congressional standing and select committees gaining TV exposure with the 1973-74 Watergate Committee and the 1987 so-called Iran-Contra hearings.

LYNDON B. JOHNSON

The 36th President of the United States was born in 1908 near Stonewall, Texas. He attended public schools and received a B.S. degree from Southwest Texas State Teachers College, San Marcos, and became a public school teacher. Two years later he accepted a position as secretary to Congressman Richard M. Kleberg.

After a year at Georgetown Law School in Washington, D.C. he became state director of the National Youth Administration of Texas. In 1937 he was elected to the 75th Congress to fill the unexpired term of Congressman James Buchanan of the Tenth District of Texas and in 1940 was reelected.

With war imminent, Johnson sought and received a commission as lieutenant commander in the Naval Reserve in June 1940. He reported for active duty at the Navy Department in Washington just three days after the Pearl Harbor attack. After a period of indoctrination at the Office of the Chief of Naval Operations he was dispatched on a fact finding tour of the Southwest Pacific, making stops in New Zealand and Australia. While at General Douglas MacArthur's

Australian headquarters he sought permission to fly on a combat mission as an observer. A mission was arranged for June 9, 1942 from Port Moresby, New Guinea.

Johnson and two other staff officers flew from Townsville, Australia on a B-17 to accompany a flight of B-26 bombers of the 22nd Bomb Group. By the luck of the draw Johnson ended up in the bomber of Lt. Walter Greer, other staff members going in different aircraft. The target was Japanese held Lae, but long before the target was reached Greer's plane developed generator trouble and he elected to abort and return to the airfield at Port Moresby. The remaining ten bombers attacked their target and were intercepted by Japanese Zero fighters. The Japanese pilots, including their famed ace, Saburo Sakai, shot down one B-26 and inflicted damage on others. One crashlanded at Port Moresby because of battle damage. One of MacArthur's staff officers was lost in the downed bomber.

The next day Johnson returned to Australia to find a Silver Star citation awaiting him, courtesy of General MacArthur. Johnson returned home

LBJ (left) as a Navy officer in Australia. The man at the far right is Brig. Gen William H. Marquat of General MacArthur's staff who accompanied Johnson on his tour to New Guinea. (Credit: President Johnson Library)

immediately and was released from active duty on July 16, 1942 based on a dictum from President Roosevelt that legislators should not serve in the armed forces. The propriety of the award remains a matter of controversy to this day.

Johnson continued his congressional career moving to the Senate in 1949. He was variously the minority or majority leader. In 1961 he was elected Vice President on the John F. Kennedy ticket and assumed the office of President upon the November 1963 assassination of JFK.

He was elected to a full term in 1964 and took office in January 1965. But because of the passions generated by the Viet Nam war he chose, in 1968, not to run for a second term.

Johnson returned to Stonewall, Texas where he ranched and wrote several political and historical works. He died there, where he had been born, on January 22, 1973.

Lt. Comdr. Lyndon B. Johnson. (Credit: President Johnson Library)

Sen. George McGovern (left) with President Lyndon Johnson. (Credit: George McGovern)

KEN KAVANAUGH

Born in Little Rock, Arkansas in 1916, he was a three-year letterman in football and baseball at Louisiana State University. He played minor league baseball in the St. Louis Cardinals organization but decided to switch to pro football when drafted by the Chicago Bears as a wide receiver.

His first years with the Bears were 1940-41, and in both they were NFL Champions.

Enlisting in the Army Air Force in 1942 he completed flight training and was assigned as a B-17 pilot with the Eighth Air Force in England. He flew 30 missions over Europe, rising to the rank of Captain, and was awarded the Distinguished Flying Cross and Air Medal with four Oak Leaf Clusters.

Returning to the Bears in 1946 he was again involved in an NFL Championship. He played until 1950, and during his eight years he made all-Pro twice. Kavanaugh still holds several Bears records: Average gain lifetime, 22.38 yards; average gain, season, 25.56;

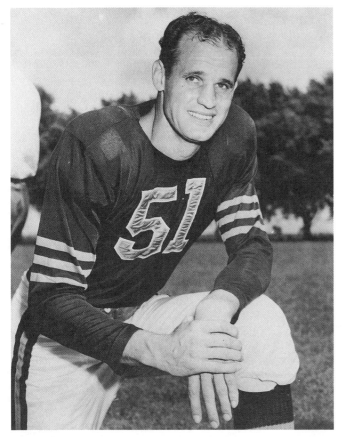

Ken Kavanaugh of the Chicago Bears. (Credit: Chicago Bears)

touchdowns, lifetime 50; touchdown, season 13 (1947). He is the number ten career receiver in the NFL and the number nine career scorer.

After his pro playing career he went into coaching: as an assistant with the Bears in 1951, Boston College 1952-53, Villanova College 1954 and the New York Giants professional team 1955-1970.

He scouted for the Giants 1n 1971 then went into business and retired to live in Fort Washington, Pennsylvania.

GENE KELLY

Born Eugene C. Kelly in 1912 in Pittsburgh, he was the son of a business executive and a former stage actress. He attended Penn State and the University of Pittsburgh supporting himself with odd jobs and as a dance instructor.

His first movie role was as part of the chorus in the 1938 Broadway musical "Leave It to Me". He got the task of being choreographer for Billy Rose's Diamond Horseshoe then moved to center stage for "Pal Joey". He choreographed "Best Foot Forward" in 1941 and then he was off to Hollywood.

Kelly's first screen role was opposite Judy Garland in the 1942 hit, **For Me and My Gal**. He worked in three more movies before joining the Navy.

During World War II he volunteered, was granted a commission in the Naval Reserve and assigned to the production of Navy documentaries while stationed in the Washington, D.C. area.

A masterful dancer, he was the successor to Fred Astaire, the screen's first King of Dance. He received an Oscar nomination for best actor in 1945's **Anchors Aweigh**, was given a Special Academy Award in 1951, and was honored with a Life Achievement Award from the Kennedy Center in 1982 and the American Film Institute in 1985.

Gene Kelly (left) with Frank Sinatra in MGM's *Anchors Aweigh,* made just after the war. (Credit: Film Favorites)

He has been involved in over 40 movies as actor, choreographer, director or producer. Some of his other fine acting roles were in: **Ziegfeld Follies, The Three Musketeers, Take Me Out to the Ball Game, An American in Paris, Singin' in the Rain, Les Girls,** and **That's Entertainment.**

He suffered a stroke in July 1994 but is recovering at his home in Beverly Hills where he lives with his third wife, Patricia Ward.

Gene Kelly, the dance king of Hollywood as he appeared in Navy uniform in WW II. (Credit: The Academy of Motion Picture Arts and Sciences)

JOHN F. KENNEDY

Born in 1917 in Brookline, Massachusetts, "Jack" Kennedy was the second son of Joe and Rose. His father, was a New England businessman and his mother was the daughter of a Boston "pol". Joesph Kennedy was appointed Ambassador to Great Britain and served in that post from 1937 to 1940, the years that saw the blossoming of World War II in Europe.

Although his father expressed some isolationist tendencies, young Jack Kennedy joined the U.S. Navy out of Harvard University and was commissioned an Ensign in 1941.

Assigned to the South Pacific he was given command of a PT boat in the Solomons Islands in mid-1943. During night operation of August 2, 1943 his boat, PT-109, was rammed and sunk by the Japanese destroyer *Amagiri*. Kennedy and his other twelve crew members were cast into the sea, many were injured and two were missing.

Despite his own severe back injury, Lieutenant Kennedy rallied his crew and, aiding the wounded, he led them to an uninhabited island. After another

Jack Kennedy in the cockpit of his vessel, PT-109, in the Solomon Islands in 1943.   (Credit: John F. Kennedy Library)

Jack Kennedy (center) was known as "Shafty" to his Navy comrades in the Solomons. They are (l. to r.) Jim Reed, Barney Ross and Red Fay. (Credit: John F. Kennedy Library)

Cliff Robertson portrayed Jack Kennedy in the Warner Bros. movie, PT 109, based on the President's WW II combat experience. (Credit: Film Favorites)

President John F. Kennedy shown here with Senator George McGovern. (Credit: George McGovern)

herculean swim, Kennedy reached another distant island where he contacted coast watchers and arranged for the rescue of his surviving crew. He was decorated with the Navy & Marine Corps Medal and the Purple Heart.

In 1953 he married Jacqueline Lee Bouvier and they had two children, Caroline and John.

Entering the presidential campaign following the two term administration of Dwight Eisenhower, Democrat Kennedy defeated Richard M. Nixon in 1960 and became the 35th President of the United States, the first Catholic elected to the office.

His first term as President was tragically terminated in November 1963 when he was assassinated in Dallas, Texas by Lee Harvey Oswald. His widow died in 1994.

JOSEPH P. KENNEDY, JR.

The oldest son of Joseph and Rose Kennedy, "Joe" graduated from Harvard in 1938. In 1940 he attended the democratic convention as a delegate from Massachusetts.

He enlisted in the U.S. Navy in June 1941, winning his wings and commission in 1942.

At first he flew anti-sub patrols in the Caribbean, then became commander of a patrol bomber of Navy Squadron VB-110. He flew 13 missions operating out of England with the RAF Coastal Command. But then he volunteered for a dangerous secret operation code named APHRODITE.

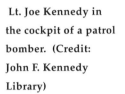

Lt. Joe Kennedy in the cockpit of a patrol bomber. (Credit: John F. Kennedy Library)

The operation focused on destruction of the heavily bunkered V-1 rocket sites in Belgium and Holland. V-1 and V-2 rockets had begun to rain down on England causing indiscriminate death and injury. They were Hitler's "reprisal" weapons for the expanding Allied bombing of Germany.

APHRODITE was a plan to impact a crewless, heavily loaded, radio guided bomber onto the launching sites. In August 1944 Lieutenant (j.g.) Joe Kennedy and his co-pilot volunteered to fly one of the heavily laden four-engine Liberator bombers from England to the Belgian coast. They were then to bail out while a following aircraft would radio control the bomber to the target. A photo chase plane was recording the event and carried Colonel Elliott Roosevelt, son of FDR. Over the North Sea Kennedy's plane mysteriously exploded, killing both crew members instantly. The cause for the tragedy was lost with the falling wreckage.

Joe Kennedy was posthumously awarded the Navy Cross

ROBERT F. KENNEDY

Born in Brookline, Massachusetts to Joe and Rose Kennedy, Bobbie attended Harvard University before entering a U.S. Navy officers V-12 flight program in 1943. The Navy cancelled Bobbie's class because of a surplus of pilots, and while he could have continued in officer candidate school he volunteered for sea duty and remained a seaman until his honorable discharge in 1946.

He served on the newly commissioned destroyer, *Joseph P. Kennedy, Jr.* named for his brother Joe who was killed in action in Europe.

Kennedy completed his B.A. at Harvard in 1948, achieved a law degree at Virginia Law School in 1951 and married Ethel Skakel in 1950.

He went to Washington, D.C. as an attorney with the Justice Department in 1951, became assistant counsel to a US. Senate subcommittee; worked on the Hoover Commission; and worked as counsel for a Senate subcommittee on labor management.

Robert became U.S. Attorney General in the administration of his brother John F. Kennedy 1961-1964. He was elected to the Senate from New York in 1965 and, in that capacity ran for the presidency himself. He was assassinated on June 6, 1968 by Sirhan Sirhan while campaigning in California.

Seaman Robert F. Kennedy (right) greets his father, Joe Kennedy, Sr. onboard the destroyer *Joseph P. Kennedy, Jr.* (Credit: John F. Kennedy Library)

RALPH KINER

Born in 1922 in Santa Rita, New Mexico, his father died when he was four and his mother, a nurse, moved to Alhambra, California to support them. As a boy he worked hard selling newspapers and delivering groceries to buy baseball equipment. His mother questioned this intense interest, but he replied, "I'll be getting a major league salary while the other guys are stuck in offices." He was such a good high school ball player that he was scouted by several major league teams. He accepted an offer from the Pittsburgh Pirates and was off to the minors. He played for two and a fraction years when World War II intervened.

Kiner joined the Navy in June 1943, entered pilot training and won his wings and a commission at Corpus Christi NAS, Texas in December 1944. He was assigned to fly the Martin PBM patrol bomber and was operating out of Kaneohe NAS, Oahu on sub patrol with Patrol Squadron 99 when the war ended. He accumulated 1,200 flying hours during his service stint which ended in December 1945 with his honorable discharge.

Returning to the Pirate organization he was brought to Pittsburgh to begin a nine year run in the outfield. He was a favorite there and turned into one of the National Leagues perennial homerun sluggers. He hit a season high of 47 homers in 1950. In 1953 the Pirates traded him to the Chicago Cubs where he played through the 1954 season. He was traded to the Cleveland Indians for 1955, his final year as an active player. He was inducted into the Hall of Fame in 1975.

He invested wisely and developed a wide range of business interests, but stayed in the public eye for many years as a radio announcer for the Chicago White Sox and then the New York Mets since 1962. He continues broadcasting Mets games while living in Connecticut and spending his winters in Palm Springs, California, with his third wife, DiAnn.

While visiting the Pensacola Naval Air Museum Ralph Kiner inspects a Catalina flying boat of the type he flew during his WW II service. (Credit: Ralph Kiner)

BURT LANCASTER

Born in New York City in 1913 as Burton Stephen Lancaster, he grew up on the Upper East Side of Manhattan. A strong healthy lad he excelled in sports and enrolled at New York University on an athletic scholarship. He quit, however, to form an acrobatic team that performed in vaudeville and touring circuses.

With the coming of World War II Lancaster enlisted in the U.S. Army, was assigned to Special Services and saw duty in North Africa and Italy. He was honorably discharged in 1945.

By a quirk of fate he got a bit part in a forgettable Broadway stage play, but he was seen by movie scouts and asked to take a small part in the 1946 movie **The Killers,** based on a Hemingway work. With that first appearance he rocketed to fame, showing not only a beautiful physique but superlative acting ability. Lancaster has appeared in some seventy films, mostly westerns, war, character studies and historic epics.

He won an Academy Award for Best Actor for **Elmer Gantry** in 1962 and received nominations for performances in **From Here to Eternity** (1953), **Birdman of Alcatraz** (1962), and **Atlantic City** (1981). Other honors include the Venice Festival Award for **Birdman of Alcatraz** and the David Donatello Award from Italy for best foreign actor for **Atlantic City.**

Some of his other notable performances were in the following films: **Brute Force** (1947), **Sorry, Wrong Number** (1948), **Jim Thorpe – All American** (1951),

Burt Lancaster (center) prepares to duke it out with Ernest Borgnine (left) in a scene from the movie, *From Here to Eternity*. Frank Sinatra is at the right. (Credit: Film Favorites)

Burt Lancaster is shown here with Deborah Kerr in the famous Hawaiian Beach scene form the movie, *From Here to Eternity*, for which Burt won an Oscar nomination. (Credit: Film Favorites)

Come Back Little Sheba (1952), **The Rose Tattoo** (1955), **Sweet Smell of Success** (1957), **The Unforgiven** (1960), **Judgement at Nuremberg** (1961), **Seven Days in May** (1964), **Airport** (1970), **Valdez is Coming** (1971), **Ulzana's Raid** (1972), **Scorpio** (1973), **The Cassandra Crossing** (1977), **Go Tell the Spartans** (1978) and **Field of Dreams** (1989).

In 1951 Lancaster formed his own production company that was responsible for several hit films. He also made movies in England, France and Italy.

Lancaster suffered a stroke in 1990 and died of complications in 1994.

TOM LANDRY

Born in Mission, Texas, he attended the University of Texas where he played football.

Landry's older brother Robert vanished over the North Atlantic while ferrying a B-17 to England early in World War II.

While still a college student he enlisted in the Army Air Force in 1942 and entered flight training. He received his wings and a commission as second lieutenant and was sent to advance schools for training on multi-engine bombers. After completion of this training he was sent to England and assigned to the 493rd Bomb Group at Ipswich. From there he flew 30 combat missions over enemy held territory in 1944. He and his crew survived a crash landing in England.

Tom Landry winning coach of the Dallas Cowboys (Credit: Tom Landry)

Resuming his education in 1946,he played football at the University of Texas and became a college football coach.

Eventually he became head coach for the Dallas Cowboys professional football team and held that position from 1960 to 1988, leading his teams to five conference championships and two superbowls.

He was inducted into the Football Hall of Fame in 1990.

CURTIS E. LEMAY

Born in Columbus, Ohio on November 15, 1906, his family was poor and moved frequently as the father sought new work. "Curt" was a serious young man who worked hard to help support the family and put himself through school. In 1924 he and a high school friend pooled five dollars for a ride with a gypsy barnstormer, and from that point on Curt wanted to be an aviator.

He entered Ohio State University, School of Engineering, in 1924 and also enrolled in the school's ROTC program. He graduated in 1928 with a reserve commission and an appointment to the Ohio National Guard. He immediately applied for the Army's new Aviation Cadet Program and was accepted, winning his wings in October 1929. He was part of a team of airmen who won the Mackey Trophy in 1937 for several long range goodwill missions.

When World War II was declared in December 1941 LeMay was a major and the operations officer for the 34th Bomb Group. Being a senior officer in the swelling ranks of the Army Air Force he was soon elevated to colonel and given his own unit to train, the 305th Bomb Group. They went to England with their B-17 Flying Fortresses to be part of the fledgling Eighth Air Force. LeMay completed a tour of combat with the 305th, winning several decorations, was promoted to brigadier general and made commander of the 3rd Bombardment Division. No sooner had he won this command than he led his Division on the infamous Schweinfurt/Regensberg mission in which 60 B-17s were lost. Despite the terrible losses from these and other deep penetration missions, LeMay became a strong advocate of strategic bombing. He was awarded

Maj. Gen. Curtis E. LeMay (Credit: USAF)

the Distinguished Service Cross, Silver Star, Air Medal and Distinguished Service Medal for his accomplishments in Europe.

As the war evolved and Boeing Aircraft Co. began to produce large quantities of the B-29 Super Fortress, successor to the B-17, Air Force strategy revolved around using this long range aircraft to attack Japan's industrial heartland. In 1944 Major General LeMay was given command of this new unit designated the 21st Bomber Command. From bases in the Marianas Islands B-29s began the 1,200 mile round trip to strike at the Japanese Home Islands. At first they employed the same high level tactics used over Germany, but LeMay was dissatisfied with results and ordered low level incendiary bombing. As the war wound to its 1945 conclusion damaged estimates for major Japanese cities were being measured in acres burned. He was award an Oak Leaf Cluster to his D.S.M.

In the postwar years LeMay led the Strategic Air Command (SAC) for nine years as it grew to become a major deterrent force in the Cold War. He attained the rank of general with four stars and assumed the top job in USAF, chief of staff, in 1961.

He retired in 1965 and went into business, then became active in politics and was running mate to Governor George Wallace in the 1972 bid for the presidency that ended with the attempted assassination and crippling of Wallace.

CHARLES A. LINDBERGH, JR.

One of America's longest standing heroes was born in Little Falls, Minnesota in 1902. His father, a Swedish immigrant was elected to the U.S. House of Representatives in the period from 1907 to 1917.

He was already a barnstormer with 330 hours fling time when he joined the Army Air Service in 1924. Upon graduation he became part of the Reserve and entered into commercial flying ventures including the air mail service. In 1927 he convinced a group of investors to acquire a Ryan aircraft for a solo attempt at flying the Atlantic. The cross-Atlantic leap was then a passion of pioneer airmen and had been tried early in May 1927 by a French team that simply vanished off the Newfoundland coast. But on May 20th "Luck Lindy" made the crossing alone in his single-engine Ryan (dubbed "Spirit of St. Louis"), departing from Long Island, New York and arriving to a cheering throng at LeBourget Airport, Paris, France.

"The Lone Eagle", as some newspaperman appropriately called him, was the toast of two continents. He had a tickertape parade in New York on his return and a fame and fortune that the quiet introverted man was unprepared to handle. In 1929 he married Ann Morrow who shared his love of flying and adventure. They lived well off Charles' various commercial flying ventures and had a son, Charles Jr.

Tragedy struck the Lindberghs as their infant son was kidnapped and killed in February 1932, an event which precipitated a celebrated trial of Bruno

Charles Lindbergh (right) in combat flying gear, 1944, talks with Maj. Tom McGuire a 38-victory ace of the 475th Fighter Group.
(Credit: McGuire AFB Archives)

Hauptman the kidnapper. Although continuing with his aviation interests Charles placed himself in a self-imposed exile from the media.

Moving for a time to Brittany to avoid the press, Charles traveled widely in Europe (partly at the behest of U.S. Army intelligence) and was warmly greeted by the international fraternity of aviators. He was hosted by the Nazi leaders as a celebrity and showered with honors by none other than Hermann Goering. Such events and Lindbergh's isolationist statements stirred controversy in the U.S. and provoked the ire of President Franklin Roosevelt. Air Corps chief Hap Arnold, however called him back to a period of active duty (with the rank of colonel) in order to be briefed on the situation in Europe.

When the Japanese struck at Pearl Harbor, Lindbergh, a reserve colonel, offered his services. Roosevelt refused to give him active duty. He sought to assist the aircraft industry or airlines, but only Henry Ford would accept him as a consultant. He worked at the Willow Run bomber plant as a $66 per month consultant and refused the money.

United Aircraft approached him to act as a technical representative for them and sent him to the Pacific in 1944 to confer with fighter units in the field regarding cruise control - ways of achieving better fuel economy and longer range. In this capacity he flew 25

missions with Marine Corsair squadrons in the Solomons, including bombing missions. The Marines began to worry about their famous consultant and he moved on (without authority) to the Army's Fifth Air Force. He participated in another 25 combat missions with the 475th Fighter Group and was engaged in a dogfight and downed a Japanese fighter on July 28, 1944. On his very next sortie he was nearly shot down.

His wartime services were not public knowledge for several years. Historians and veterans were the ones who revealed the information. A man who could have played on his own fame, Charles Lindbergh never did that. He loathed anything that smacked of public relations, a fact that constantly had him in hot water with journalists.

Lindbergh became something of a recluse in the postwar years, working as a sometime consultant for Pan American Airways but mostly spending his time with Anne and his four children at his home in Hana, Maui. He died and was buried there in 1974.

JOE LOUIS

Born in 1914 as Joseph Louis Barrow, he became one of the most celebrated boxers in American history, the best heavyweight in the history of boxing according to some experts.

Sgt. Joe Louis visits a bomber base in Italy during his tour of the European Theatre of war. (Credit: George Kay)

Called the "Brown Bomber," he turned pro in 1934 and won his title in 1935. He defended it 25 times, fighting until 1951. In that span of time his boxing earnings reached near four million.

Two of his most famous fights were against German heavyweight chap, Max Schmeling who was one of Hitler's propaganda profiles representing the "Master Race".

Louis was drafted in the U.S. Army in January 1942 and served his military duty performing boxing demonstrations for U.S. troops both in the States and overseas. He was honorably discharged in 1945 at the rank of sergeant.

United Artists made a movie of the great fighter's life, **The Joe Louis Story**, with Coley Wallace playing Joe.

Joe Louis died in Las Vegas, Nevada in 1981.

Tonight's Displays

with

Sgt. JOE LOUIS

will be

Sgt. GEORGE NICHOLSON

The Champions sparring partner since 1937   (NEW YORK)

and

Sgt. JAMES (California Jackie) WILSON

Ranked as America's No. 2 Welterweight   (LOS ANGELSE)

In addition to this "act" an Amateur Match between Two American Air Force Teams which Joe Louis may referee.

A poster advertising a Joe Louis exhibition match in England. (Credit: George Kay)

Movie poster for Louis' film biography. (Credit: Film Favorites)

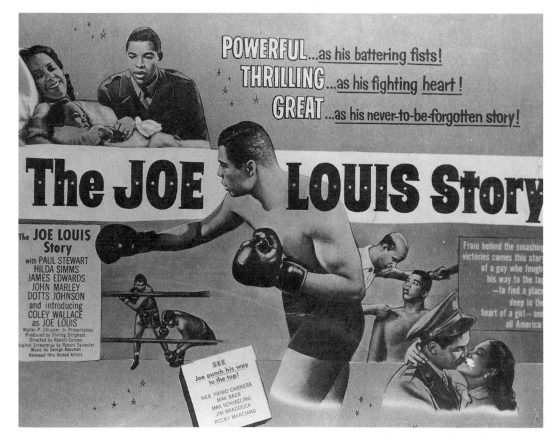

DOUGLAS MACARTHUR

This future five-star general was the son of Lieutenant General Arthur and Mary MacArthur, born on January 26, 1880.

Following in his fathers footsteps he graduated from the U.S. Military Academy in 1903 and received successive honorary degrees from Pennsylvania Military College, the University of Maryland, the University of Western Maryland, University of Pittsburgh, the University of Wisconsin, the University of the Philippines, Queensland University (Australia), Harvard, Columbia and the University of Seoul (Korea).

As Chief of Staff of the 34th (Rainbow) Division he served with distinction in World War I in France. He was highly decorated and won a reputation for his fearlessness.

He returned to West Point as Superintendent of the Military Academy between 1919 and 1922 and achieved the rank of General in 1930. During this period between the World Wars MacArthur gained unwanted notoriety as the military leader forced to disperse an army of unemployed who had marched on the capitol of Washington, DC.

Gen. Douglas MacArthur. (Credit: Lambert Archives)

A movie about the wartime exploits of Douglas MacArthur starred Gregory Peck, seen here reenacting the return to Luzon. (Credit: Film Favorites)

In 1935 MacArthur returned to the Philippines, where his father had been stationed when Douglas was a boy. Both the U.S. and the Philippine governments, concerned over growing Japanese belligerence in Asia, sought to use MacArthur to build the defenses of the Philippines. He was accorded the rank of Field Marshall of the Philippine Army. His wife Jean accompanied him and their only child, Arthur was born there.

When the Japanese plunged the U.S. into war on December 7, 1941 with the Pearl Harbor attack, they also raided military installations on Luzon and invasion was imminent. MacArthur was named commander of all U.S. and Filipino forces. As the Japanese swept through Allied military strongholds such as Hong Kong, Malaya, Singapore and the Dutch East Indies, MacArthur's outgunned forces gave ground grudgingly with a courageous defense. For five months they held out on an ever shrinking perimeter in the Bataan Peninsular, a defense that made MacArthur and his "Battling Bastards of Bataan" famous in America. As the inevitable end drew near for the Philippine Army, President Roosevelt ordered MacArthur to escape to Australia. A flamboyant leader and spellbinding speaker, MacArthur captured the hearts of Americans on the home front with his dispatches and final declaration on departing the Philippines, "I shall return."

From Australia he rallied Allied forces and began the long, grueling island hopping march back to the Philippines and to the very doorstep of Japan. Military historians considered his campaigns tactically brilliant, although troops serving under him were of a mixed view. At the defeat of the Japanese Government, General Mac Arthur presided over the surrender ceremony on board the Battleship *Missouri*.

General MacArthur (seated) at the surrender ceremony in Tokyo Bay aboard battleship *Missouri*. (Credit: Campbell Archives)

As commander of U.S. forces in the Far East, he managed the reconstruction of the Japanese government along democratic lines and was instrumental in the economic recovery of that war ravaged nation. His enlightened administration of Japan resulted in his being revered by the Japanese.

When North Korea attacked the Republic of South Korea in June 1950, MacArthur was designated commander of all United Nations forces. He engineered a brilliant back door invasion at Inchon, which served to cut off North Korean forces from their supply sources. Pursuing the defeated Army north into their home territory MacArthur's forces reached the Yalu River, the border with Red China, and this precipitated the entry of that nation's vast Army on the side of the North Koreans.

MacArthur's determination to fight the Chinese and bomb their supply bases in China led to a strategy disagreement with then President Harry Truman who feared that such military actions would widen the war possibly even bringing Russian forces to the aid of their Chinese and North Korean allies. In a 1951 MacArthur was relieved of his command and ordered back to the United States by Truman.

He returned home to general public acclamation and in some cases ticker-tape parades. He delivered many speeches concerning his view of the Communist menace in Asia and there was talk of drafting him for the presidency. However, Dwight Eisenhower became the Republican candidate in 1952.

It may be that he is the most decorated American soldier of the century with the following awards from three wars: Medal of Honor, Distinguished Service Cross with two clusters, Distinguished Service Medal with six clusters, Silver Star with six clusters, Distinguished Service Medal (Navy), Distinguished Flying Cross, Air Medal, Purple Heart with one cluster, Bronze Star Medal, and seventeen foreign awards.

General MacArthur lived out his remaining years as a board member for the Sperry Rand Corp. and as a public speaker. His most famous line, delivered at West Point, "Old soldiers never die, they just fade away," became a popular ballad. He died in 1964 in Virginia.

KARL MALDEN

Born Mladen Sekulovich in 1913 in Chicago, Malden attended Chicago's Goodman Theatre Dramatic School and began acting on the Broadway stage in 1937. He had performed in just one movie before the start of World War II. In 1938 he married actress Mona Graham.

He joined the U.S. Army Air Force in 1943 and after assignment to a service unit participated in "Winged Victory" along with Red Buttons, Edmond O'Brien and others who would gain show business fame.

Back from the military in 1945 he returned to films making three in 1947: **13 Rue Madeleine**, **Boomerang** and **Kiss of Death**. He was often cast as a "heavy" in early films and won an Oscar for his supporting performance in **Streetcar Named Desire** (1951) and a nomination for his role in **On the Waterfront**.

Malden continued to appear as a major character actor in a variety of complex film roles: **The Hanging Tree** (1959), **Gypsy** (1962),**Cheyenne Autumn** (1964), **Patton** (1970), **Summertime Killer** (1973), **Beyond the Poseidon Adventure** (1979) and **Nuts**.

Simultaneously he took a leap into television with "The Streets of San Francisco" crime series 1972 to 1977. He won an Emmy for his performance in the TV movie, "Fatal Vision" from 1984.

He achieved additional celebrity as a TV pitchman for American Express with their long running, "Don't Leave Home Without It" commercials. Between 1989 and 1993 the highly respected Malden served as president of the Academy of Motion Picture Arts and Sciences.

Karl Malden appears (left) in the movie, *Patton*, as Lt. Gen. Omar Bradley. Right is George C. Scott as Maj. Gen. Patton. (Credit: Film Favorites)

LEE MARVIN

Born in New York City in 1924, he attended schools in New York and Florida before enlisting in the Marines at 19.

Joining the Corps in 1943, he was sent to the Pacific early in 1944 and assigned to I Company, 3rd Battalion, 24th Regiment, 4th Marine Division as a rifleman. He was involved in the invasion of Saipan in the Marianas Islands in June 1918 and was seriously wounded, receiving the Purple Heart and a Unit Commendation Medal. After extensive hospitalization he was invalided out of the Marine Corps in 1945.

He was working at odd jobs when asked to perform as a substitute in summer stock. After that experience he took up acting seriously, schooling at New York's American Theatre Wing before several off-Broadway appearances. He made it to Broadway in 1951 and got his first film role the same year.

Marvin seldom played a romantic role. He was usually in war or western dramas, frequently the bad guy. However, he won comedy fame for his hilarious performance in the 1963 movie **Cat Ballou** opposite Jane Fonda.

Lee Marvin (foreground) in the post war film, *Hell in the Pacific*. (Credit: Film Favorites)

He also ventured into television with a series titled "M-Squad" that ran from 1957 to 1960.

Some of the other films for which he will be remembered are: **Hangman's Knot** (1953), **Bad Day at Black Rock** and **Pete Kelly's Blues** (1955), **Raintree County** (1957), **The Comancheros** (1961), **The Man Who Shot Liberty Valance** (1962), **The Dirty Dozen** (1967), **Hell in the Pacific** (1968), **Monte Walsh** (1970), **Prime Cut** (1972), **The Big Red One** (1980) and his last, **The Delta Force** in 1986.

Marvin gained some unwanted fame and set legal precedent in 1979 when his former live-in woman friend sued him for alimony. The California court ruling established the "palimony doctrine".

Marvin died of a heart attack in 1987 leaving his wife, Pamela.

Lee Marvin, the actor and Oscar winner. (Credit: Mrs. Pamela Marvin)

Lee Marvin as the grizzled sergeant in the film, *The Big Red One*. (Credit: Film Favorites)

WALTER MATTHAU

Born Walter Matuschanskavasky in 1920 of Jewish-Russian immigrant parents. He grew up on New York's Lower East Side. His first association with the arts was as a boy pop peddler in a Yiddish theatre. He began to play bit roles and thus became bitten by the acting bug, but worked in several menial jobs before World War II.

He enlisted in the Army Air Force in April 1942 and, after training, was sent to England assigned to the 453rd Bomb Group. He was an technician but managed to fly four combat missions and attained the rank of sergeant. He said that he was the self-proclaimed ping-pong champion of Europe.

Returning from the war Matthau shuffled between Broadway and Hollywood seeking work. He made his first movie in 1955, **The Kentuckian**, and usually played the role of a villain.

Walter Matthau as he appeared in the movie, *Fail Safe*, one of his rare dramatic roles. (Credit: Film Favorites)

However, in 1965 he achieved stardom in Neil Simon's Broadway comedy "The Odd Couple", a role that was recreated with co-star Jack Lemmon in the movie of the same title. The movie was such a hit that it spawned a TV series (but without Matthau).

In 1966 he won a supporting actor Oscar for **The Fortune Cookie.** This honor was followed by Academy Award nominations for best actor in **Kotch** (1971) and **The Sunshine Boys** (1975). These and other efforts have established him as one of Hollywood's comic geniuses.

Matthau has made over 50 films. Some of his other memorable performances were in: **Ensign Pulver, Plaza Suite, Hello Dolly, The Bad News Bears, The Taking of Pelham One Two Three, Little Miss Marker,** and **JFK 1991.**

VICTOR J. MATURE

Born in Kentucky in 1915, future screen star Victor Mature attended primary and secondary schools in Kentucky, the Kentucky Military Institute and Spenserian Business School. He worked at a variety of odd jobs before moving to California and attending the Pasadena Community Playhouse a drama school.

He made his stage debut in 1936 in **Paths of Glory** and broke into movies in 1939 with a role in **The Housekeeper's Daughter**. In 1939 he won a leading role in MGM's **One Million B.C.**, which propelled him to Broadway for the stage play, **Lady in the Dark.**

Victor Mature as he appeared in the movie, *Tank Force*. (Credit: Film Favorites)

Mature enlisted in the United States Coast Guard in 1942 and served as an enlisted man on ships in both the North Atlantic and the Pacific until his honorable discharge in 1945.

In the immediate postwar era he portrayed Doc Holliday in **My Darling Clementine** (1946), a western, then saw several starring roles in ancient epics such as **Samson and Delilah** and **Land of the Pharaohs**. During a long film career he participated in just one war movie, **Tank Force**.

Mature retired in the 1960s and lives in Rancho Santa Fe, California.

GEORGE S. MC GOVERN

Born in Avon, South Dakota on July 19, 1922, he married Eleanor Stegeberg in 1943.

He joined the Army Air Force and completed flight training in 1943. Assigned to the 741st Bomb Squadron, 455th Bomb Group in the Mediterranean Theatre of Operations flying B-24 Liberator four-engined bombers, Mc Govern's aircraft was named "Dakota Queen". He flew 35 missions and on his 30th

A candid photo of Lt. George McGovern and his wife, Eleanor, before he left for overseas. (Credit: George McGovern)

A Liberator bomber. George McGovern, Lloyd Bentsen, Joe Kennedy and Sabu all served in this type. (Credit: Van Osdol Archives)

was forced down on Viz, an island in the Adriatic Sea controlled by Tito's Yugoslavian partisans. He was awarded the Distinguished Flying Cross and the Air Medal with three clusters.

Senator George McGovern. (Credit: George McGovern)

After the war he received his B.A. at Dakota Weslyan University, his Masters Degree at Northwestern University and his PhD. He returned to Weslyan as a professor of political science 1949-53.

Entering South Dakota politics first, he ran for and won a seat in the U.S. House of Representatives, then he won a U.S. Senate seat in 1963. He was an unsuccessful Democratic candidate for the presidency in 1972.

He lives and practices law in the Washington D.C. area.

ED MCMAHON

One of televisions most recognizable faces and voices, McMahon was born in 1923. He joined the Naval Aviation Cadet Program on February 9, 1943, trained in Texarkana, Texas, Athens, Georgia and Dallas, Texas before winning his wings and a commission in the United States Marines.

In August 1944 he qualified in fighters and was made an instructor and later a test pilot. At the end of the war he was placed on inactive duty in April 1946 but remained in the reserves.

He started his show business career as a circus clown on "Big Top" in 1950.

Recalled to active duty in 1951 for the Korean war he was assigned to the First Marine Division as an artillery spotter and forward air controller. McMahon flew an L-19 over the ground combat zone in Korea during 85 missions and was awarded the Air Medal with six Oak Leaf Clusters. He was released from active duty and reassigned to the reserves in 1952.

Resuming his career in television he first linked up with Johnny Carson in the 1957-63 daytime quiz show, "Who Do You Trust?". He hosted three daytime game shows in in the 1960s and 1970s before starting his long run with Carson on the "Tonight" show. Since that marvelously successful venture he has also co-hosted "TV Bloopers & Practical Jokes" with Dick Clark, as well as hosting "Star Search".

He remained active in the Marine Corps for 23 years retiring on his 60th birthday as a colonel.

Ed McMahon. (Credit: Ed McMahon)

A liaison plane similar to that flown by McMahon in Korea. (Credit: Van Osdol Archives)

GLENN MILLER

Alton G. Miller, was born in 1904 in Clarinda, Iowa and in a relatively short lifetime left a legacy of fine music that has been enjoyed to this day.

In an era of "big band" sounds - the Dorseys, Artie Shaw, Kay Kaiser - none was more idolized than the music of the Glenn Miller band.

With a strong sense of patriotism Miller began his "'Sunset Serenade" Saturday radio broadcasts with prizes of records and a radio/phonograph combination for military camps. This was in August 1941, three months before Pearl Harbor, when military posts were being swelled by the draft. The shows were later incorporated into the Chesterfield program broadcasts, and during its course, until September 24, 1942, over 11,000 records and sixty-nine radio/phonograph combinations had been donated.

But long before this Glenn had begun his campaign to join the colors, although his band was at the height of its popularity and was grossing $15,000 to $20,000 per week - a kings ransom for 1942. First

the married 38 year old applied to and was rejected by the Navy. He applied to the Army and in due course they decided he would be an asset. Glenn was commissioned a Captain in the Air Force in December 1942 and immediately formed a service band that played at what were largely military functions. It was during this period that he added some zip to the music by arranging the "St. Louis Blues March". The band also did a radio program entitled, "I Sustain the Wings", the motto of the Training Command.

In June 1944 the Glenn Miller Band sailed for the war and set up shop amid the Buzz Bombs that the Germans were raining on England. They did both regular radio broadcasts and over 40 appearances at military bases in the period from July 8 to October 3. Later they played regularly at the Queensbury All-Services Club.

But the war and the fighting were moving across the Continent and Miller campaigned to bring his band to the front. On December 12, 1944 Miller took off from Southern England in a single-engine Norseman utility transport bound for Paris, where he planned to

A publicity still from the musical, *Sun Valley Serenade*, that featured Glenn Miller and orchestra, along with Sonja Henie and John Payne. (Credit: Film Favorites)

make arrangements for his band that would follow. The plane never arrived and no trace was ever found, suggesting that it likely fell into the English Channel.

In eulogizing Miller, Lieutenant General Jimmy Doolittle said, "Next to letters from home, the Glenn Miller Army Band was the greatest morale builder we had in the European Theater of Operations."

Miller's memory was enhanced by the 1953 film, **The Glenn Miller Story**, in which Jimmy Stewart played the maestro. Miller's music lived on long after he was gone and, thanks to recordings, is continuously enjoyed by new generations.

A performance at Boxted, England. (Credit: 56th FG)

The Glenn Miller band at Knettishall, England. (Credit: Ed Huntzinger)

Zeke Zachary is at the mike for a trumpet solo at Steeple-Morden, England. (Credit: 355th FG)

Performing outdoors on a flatbed truck trailer, Bobby Nichols is doing a trumpet solo at Podington, England. (Credit: 92nd BG)

The Glenn Miller band performs at a celebration of the 200th mission at Horam, England home of the 95th Bomb Group. (Credit: 95th BG)

The band performing with the:"Crew Chiefs" at the mike on the vocal for "Juke Box Saturday Night", at Thorpe Abbots, base of the 100th Bomb Group. (Credit: 100 BG)

Swinging out with "In the Mood" at Thorpe Abbots, England. (Credit: 100th BG)

With the band performing and the "Crew Chiefs" singing, the audience is literally swinging from the rafters at Wendling, England. (Credit: 392nd BG)

The band takes a break to watch Ray McKinley on a drum solo at Podington, England, August 1944. (Credit: 92nd BG)

Capt. Glenn Miller, August 6, 1944, at Halesworth, England. (Credit: 489th BG)

ROBERT MONTGOMERY

One of America's most suave, debonair actors was born Henry Montgomery in Beacon, New York in 1921.

He had hoped to become a writer, but after repeated failures he tried acting and made his Broadway stage debut in 1924. His career was well established when he made the move to Hollywood in 1929.

With MGM he made the light romantic movies that were main fare in the era of the 30s, playing opposite the glamour queens of the day. He was nominated for Oscars for **Night Must Fall** (1937) and **Here Comes Mr. Jordan** (1941). Some of his early screen credits included: **The Big House** (1930), **Strangers May Kiss** (1931), **Biography of a Bachelor** (1935), **Yellow Jack** (1938), **The Earl of Chicago** (1940), and **Rage in Heaven** (1941).

Moved by the war in Europe, he went to Paris in 1940 and served as an ambulance driver with American Field Services. As the Nazi Blitzkrieg overran the low countries and France he returned to the United States.

In August 1941, prior to America's entry into the war, Montgomery enlisted in the Navy and was granted a commission as lieutenant (junior grade), and

One of Robert Montomery's post war roles was in *They Were Expendable*. He is shown here with John Wayne and Donna Reed in that movie. (Credit: Film Favorites)

Lt. Comdr. Robert Montgomery and wife, Elizabeth Bryan Allen, on his return from WW II. (Credit: The Academy of Motion Picture Arts and Sciences)

was sent to the Embassy in London where he observed the Blitz, returning in November 1941. Montgomery trained as a ships officer and was assigned to a PT-boat squadron in the Solomons. After several months there he contracted malaria and returned to the States.

He was next assigned to a destroyer of the Atlantic Fleet as operations officer and participated in the D-Day invasion. He was awarded the Bronze Star for his actions in that operation, and in 1947 the French Government honored his volunteer service as an ambulance driver with the Legion of Honor.

Returning to the film capital, Montgomery immediately tried his hand at directing, subbing for an ill John Ford on the set of **They Were Expendable**, a 1945 movie in which he also acted. In 1947 he did the acting/directing again in **Lady in the Lake**.

Montgomery only made seven postwar films. However, he was a busy man involving himself in conservative politics for Tom Dewey and Dwight Eisenhower. He also produced, directed, hosted (and occasionally acted) in the TV drama series "Robert Montgomery Presents" which ran from 1950-1957. With Jimmy Cagney he produced and directed **The Gallant Hours** in 1960, his swan song as a director.

During the 1960s as a businessman he served as communications consultant to several clients and was on the board of Macys, the Milwaukee Telephone Company and the Lincoln Center for the Performing Arts.

He died in 1981, and his daughter Elizabeth Montgomery carried on his acting tradition with, among other shows, the TV series "Bewitched."

WAYNE MORRIS

Born Bert de Wayne Morris in 1917, he was a native of Los Angeles and began his acting career at the Pasadena Playhouse.

In the era of tall, dark leading men, Morris was an anomoly, the blond all-American type. He broke into

films in 1936 with **China Clipper** and received good reviews for the 1937 production, **Kid Galahad**. He had performed in eighteen films when World War II broke.

Morris enlisted in the Navy, completed flight training, won his wings and was assigned to a carrier

A movie publicity shot for *Flight Angels*, starring (left to right) Wayne Morris, Jane Wyman (later Mrs. Ronald Reagan), Virginia Bruce and Dennis Morgan. (Credit: Film Favorites)

A movie poster promoting one of Wayne Morris' Republic roles. (Credit: Film Favorites.

CROSS CHANNEL

starring

Wayne Morris · Yvonne Furneaux

with **Arnold Marle · Peter Sinclair · Carl Jaffe**

fighter squdron in the Pacific. Flying a Grumman F6F Hellcat fighter of Fighting Squadron 15 from the aircraft carrier *Essex*, he destroyed seven Japanese planes in aerial combat and probably destroyed another. In addition he assisted in the sinking of of an enemy patrol craft and two destroyers.

He was discharged from the Navy in 1945 with the rank of lieutenant commander, having been awarded the Distinguished Flying Cross and three clusters and the Air Medal with two clusters for valor during his 57 combat missions.

He returned to films almost immediately and some of his postwar starring roles were: **The Voice of the Turtle** (1947), **The Time of Your Life** (1948), **Johnnie One-Eye** (1950), **The Marksman** (1953), **The Deperado** (1954) and **Paths of Glory** (1957). His last movie, **Buffalo Gun**, was not released until 1961.

Morris retained his interest in the Navy and was attending an aerial display aboard an aircraft carrier when he died of a heart attack in 1959 at the age of 45. He had performed in a total of 47 movies in the U.S. and England.

Wayne Morris climbs into the cockpit of his Grumman F6F Hellcat fighter. The Japanese flags represent Wayne's seven aerial victories in Pacific combat. (Credit: US Navy)

AUDIE MURPHY

Born in Texas in 1924 of a poor farm family, he had trouble enlisting because of his small frame and boyish appearance.

However, he managed to join the U.S. Army at the age of 19 and after being shipped to Italy became the most decorated American soldier of World War II. He received 24 citations for bravery in the face of the enemy and as a consequence was awarded the Congressional Medal of Honor, the Distinguished Service Cross, the Silver Star with two clusters, the Bronze Star, the Purple Heart with two clusters, The Legion of Merit and the French Legion of Honor.

Joining the Army as private he rose through the enlisted ranks and was awarded a battle field commission for his extraordinary leadership and bravery. At the end of World War II he was a national hero.

He turned his boyish good looks into an acting career on his return from the war, many of his films being adventure, war or westerns. He appeared in 46 films starting in 1948. Some of them are: **The Kid From Texas** (1950), **The Red Badge of Courage** (1951), **Drums Across the River** (1954), **To Hell and Back,** Audie's own war experience (1955), **Ride A Crooked Trail** (1958), **Cast a Long Shadow** (1959), **The Unforgiven** (1960),

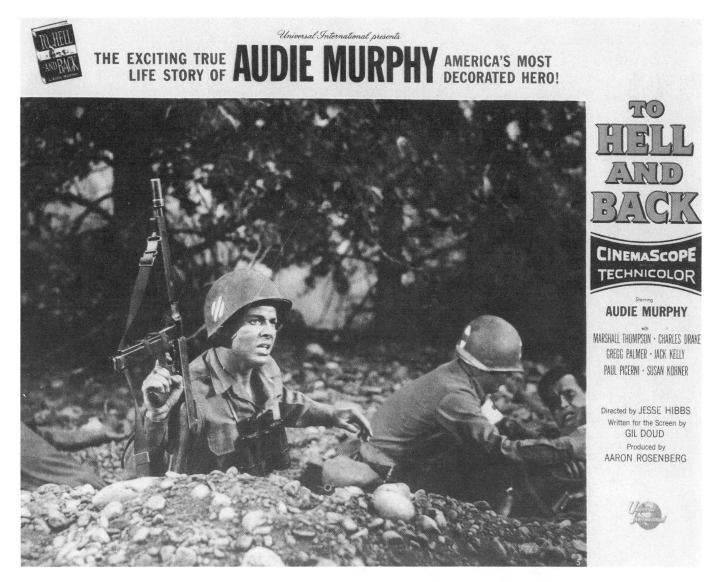

A publictity poster for the movie on Audie Murphy's life, *To Hell and Back*, starring Audie Murphy in the role he lived. (Credit: Film Favorites)

A film clip from the movie, *Battle at Bloody Beach*, staring Audie Murphy. (Credit: Film Favorites)

Gunfight at Comanche Creek (1964), **The Texican** (1966) and his last, **A Time For Dying** (1971).

Murphy had marital and then money problems in his career and was struggling with a financial comeback when he was killed in a 1971 plane crash. He was buried with full military honors in Arlington National Cemetery.

STAN MUSIAL

Born in 1920 in Donora, Pennsylvania, he became known to baseball fans as "Stan the Man".

As a rookie he broke in with the St. Louis Cardinals as an outfielder in 1941 and played until 1944 when he was called to service.

Stan was in the U.S. Navy from 1944 until his honorable discharge in 1946. He was assigned to a Special Service Unit and participated in sporting events and bond drives.

Returning to the Cards, he played with that team until his retirement in 1964 in the outfield or first base position. During his career he played in four world series, batted .331 lifetime, and hit 475 homeruns. He was elected to the Hall of Fame in 1959.

In his retirement, Musial became a restaurateur (Stan & Biggies) in St. Louis.

Stan the Man Musial in his Navy duds during WW II. (Credit: National Baseball Library, Cooperstown, NY)

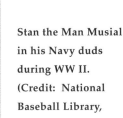

PAUL NEWMAN

Newman was born in 1925 in Cleveland, the son of Jewish and Catholic parents. He was educated at Shaker Heights High School and Kenyon College in Bambier, Ohio and at the Yale Drama School in New Haven, Connecticut.

At the outset of World War II he enlisted in the Navy and had hoped for flight training, but this was denied because of some eye problem. He was trained as a radioman/gunner and served in the Pacific in a torpedo squadron. He was honorably discharged in 1946.

He performed in repertory theater in Wisconsin and Illinois then returned to Cleveland to help with the family sporting goods business until 1952. After a stint in New York television he appeared in a stage production of "Picnic" and this led to a screen contract.

His first movie was **Silver Chalice** in 1955, followed by forty years of starring roles. He won the Cannes Film Festival award for **The Long Hot Summer** (1958) and an Oscar nomination for Best Actor for **Cat On a Hot Tin Roof** in the same year. He was nominated several more times for Oscars: **The Hustler** (1961), **Hud** (1963), **Cool Hand Luke** (1967), **Absence of Malice** (1981) and **The Verdict** (1982). He finally won his Oscar for **The Color of Money** in 1986.

Newman's good looks, piercing blue eyes and intelligent grasp of each role have made him a favorite with movie audiences to this day. He has appeared in over 60 films. Some of his other memorable movies are: **Butch Cassidy and the Sundance Kid, The Sting, Slap Shot, Fort Apache the Bronx, Blaze** and **Mr. & Mrs. Bridge.**

He continues to act, direct and produce films, write books, race cars, and maintain his interest in the food business. He is married to noted actress Joanne Woodward.

Paul Newman in a clinch from the movie, *The Silver Chalice.* (Credit: Film Favorites)

CHESTER W. NIMITZ

Born in Fredericksburg, Texas in 1885, he graduated from the U.S. Naval Academy in 1905 and married Catherine Vance Freeman in 1913.

He saw submarine duty in the Atlantic during World War I and rose through grades and was a vice admiral in the Navy Department at the start of World War II.

Unknown to the general public, Nimitz took command of the beleaguered Pacific Fleet shortly after the Japanese attack on Pearl Harbor, December 7, 1941. He shared Pacific Theatre command with General Douglas MacArthur, Nimitz dealing with the vast Central and Southern Pacific. The stunning U.S. Navy victories from Midway (June 1942) onward reflected the brilliant strategy of Chester Nimitz. Made Admiral of the Fleet in 1944, he was present at the Japanese surrender in Tokyo Bay on the Battleship, *Missouri*.

After the war he became Chief of Naval Operations until 1947 when he retired from active duty. His decorations include: Distinguished Service Medal and one Gold Star, D.S.M. (Army), and the Silver Life Saving Medal. He has been honored with awards from thirteen foreign countries and received many honorary degrees.

He died in 1966.

RICHARD M. NIXON

Born on a lemon ranch in Yorba Linda, California in 1913, Nixon was educated in Whittier, California, graduating from Whittier College with a B.A. He graduated from Duke University Law School in 1937 and was admitted to the California bar, marrying Patricia Ryan in 1940.

Admiral of the Fleet Chester Nimitz. (Credit: Admiral Nimitz Museum)

Lt. Richard Nixon in the Southwest Pacific, 1944. (Credit: President Richard Nixon Library)

Lt. Comdr. Richard Nixon at war's end. (Credit: President Richard Nixon Library)

When World War II broke out he volunteered and received a commission in the U.S. Naval Reserve as a lieutenant, junior grade and was assigned to the South Pacific. As a member of the Air Transport Command, Nixon served on a number of island outposts from June 1943 to August 1944. He was discharged from the Navy in January 1946 having attained the rank of lieutenant commander.

That same year he began his political career, winning election to the House of Representatives from the 12th Congressional District of California. He ran for and was elected to the Senate of the United States in 1950. Just two years later he became Vice President as a member of the Eisenhower ticket.

Despite early political victories, Nixon tasted defeat in bids for the presidency in 1960 and the governorship of California in 1962. He returned to private law practice but maintained a following in the Republican Party and as their nominee was elected the 37th President of the United States in November 1968.

He left the Presidency in 1974, during his second term, as a result of the Watergate scandal, resigning in favor of Vice-President Gerald Ford. Between his law practice and foreign travels, often at the behest of various presidential administrations, Nixon maintained a vigorous schedule until his death in 1994.

HUGH O'BRIAN

Born Hugh J. Krampke in Rochester, New York in 1925, he was raised in the Chicago area attending school in Winnetka and Kemper Military Academy in Booneville, Missouri. He was a four letter athlete in high school. After a semester at Cincinnati University with pre-law studies he enlisted in the Marine Corps at age 17. His father was a Marine.

World War II was underway but the Corps kept him at boot camp as a drill instructor. During his four year service the Corps granted him a rare enlisted fleet appointment to the U.S. Naval Academy. He declined the honor, intending to continue his law studies at Yale.

On receiving his honorable discharge he went to Los Angeles planning to earn college tuition money. There he met budding actresses Ruth Roman and Linda Christian who introduced him to an amateur theatre group. When a leading man became ill O'Brian agreed to substitute and received such good reviews that he decided to enroll at UCLA and continue his stage work as an avocation. Established actress Ida Lupino saw one of O'Brian's performances and signed him for a

Sgt. Hugh O'Brian. (Credit: Judi Hixson, Hugh O'Brian Foundation)

repertory roll in a play she was directing. With this success and the contacts he was in films by 1950.

Some of his movies were: **The Return of Jesse James, Little Big Horn, Meet Me at the Fair, Battle of Apache Pass, Back to God's Country, Broken Lance, Come Fly With Me, In Harm's Way, Ambush Bay** and **Killer Force.**

O'Brian has acted in some 34 movies, largely westerns, but his greatest success was in TV with a popular series based on the character of Wyatt Earp, "The Life and Legend of Wyatt Earp" that ran for six years from 1955-61 with endless syndications. The series made him a wealthy man and he invested wisely. He is well known for his charitable work, specifically the founding of the Hugh O'Brian Youth Foundation, for which O'Brian has received many honors.

Hugh O'Brian, his Marine dad, mother and younger brother. (Credit: Judi Hixson, Hugh O'Brian Foundation)

JACK PALANCE

Born on February 18, 1919, in Lattimer, Pennsylvania as Walter Jack Palahnuik, the son of a coal miner, he attended the University of North Carolina and Stanford. He was an athlete and a pro-boxer.

In World War II he joined the Air Force, completed flight school and won his wings. Assigned to train in B-24 four-engine bombers, Palance was involved in a fiery crash in Arizona. He was severely injured requiring reconstructive surgery, a fact that contributed to the ruggedness of his highly recognizable features.

He spent several years on stage before appearing in a Hollywood film, **Panic in the Streets**, in 1950. For a long time he was type cast as a sinister character but was soon recognized as a superb actor. He was nominated for Best Supporting Actor award for **Sudden Fear** in 1952 and **Shane** a year later.

Working for film makers in Hollywood, Mexico, France, Italy, Germany, England and Japan he has appeared in 70 movies. Despite that vigorous schedule he found time for considerable TV work, starring in **The Greatest Show on Earth** from 1963 to 1964, **Bronk** 1975 to 1976; and movies made for TV, **Requiem for a Heavyweight** (1956) and **Dracula** (1973). He won an

Jack Palance in a scene from the movie, *Attack*. (Credit: Film Favorites)

Emmy for **Requiem**. Palance was host of the **Ripley's Believe it or Not** show for five years in the mid-80s. Adding to these statistics and his past laurels, he won an Oscar as Best Supporting Actor for the movie **City Slickers** in 1991, entertaining the Academy and TV audience with one-armed pushups on stage. He performed in the sequel, **City Slickers II,** in 1994.

Married but twice divorced, he has a son and daughter in the acting profession. Palance lives on his working cattle ranch in the Tehachapi area of California.

A movie poster pitches *Attack*. (Credit: Film Favorites)

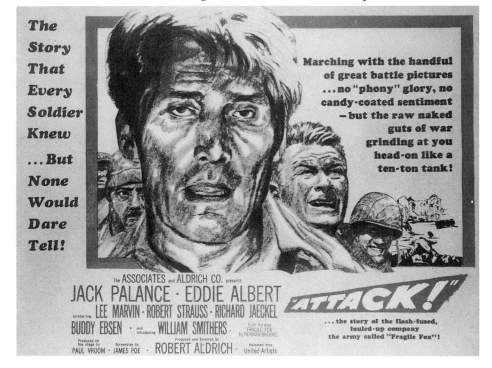

GEORGE S. PATTON

Born in San Gabriel, California on November 11, 1885, he attended Virginia Military Institute and the U.S. Military Academy at West Point graduating as a second lieutenant of cavalry in 1909.

Rising through the ranks and various assignments, the Mexican Expedition of 1916 found him as an aide to General John Pershing. With the outbreak of World War I he accompanied Pershing to France saw extensive combat, was wounded and highly decorated.

Between the wars he was a strong advocate of highly mobile tank warfare, and the outbreak of World War II for the U.S. found him in command of the 2nd Armored Division at Fort Benning, Georgia.

With the Allied invasion of North Africa in November 1942, Major General Patton was placed in command of all U.S. ground forces. He campaigned in North Africa and then in Sicily as head of the Third Army. A flamboyant military genius, who was frequently at the front in the midst of battle, he got into trouble with the high command an the American public for an incident wherein he slapped a man he thought to be malingering in a field hospital. General Dwight Eisenhower relieved Patton of his command for a time, but with the invasion of France looming, Ike restored him and placed him at the head of the Third Army.

His performance in France in 1944 was brilliant and his forces were thrusting for the heart of Germany when, in mid-December, the Germans launched the Battle of the Bulge in the Ardennes. Patton's Army, south of the salient, wheeled north and struck the German flank halting the enemy drive. He also relieved beleaguered U.S. troops in Bastogne, Belgium, then helped to rout the German force. With the arrival of the new year, 1945, Patton's Army again drove toward the German border outracing other Allied Armies and was the first to cross the Rhine and the first to reach a German concentration camp.

On viewing the horrifying scene and the handful of pitiful survivors at Buchenwald, Patton was so infuriated that he force marched the civilian population from the nearby town to witness camp conditions.

Maj. Gen. George S. Patton (left center) prepares to go ashore during the invasion of French Morocco, North Africa, November 1942. (Credit: Lambert Archives)

With the war over, and at the peak of his success, commanding the 15th Army in France, he died in a bizarre auto accident on December 21, 1945.

He was one of America's most highly decorated soldiers winning the Medal of Honor, Distinguished Service Cross with Cluster, the Silver Star with Cluster, Purple Heart, the Bronze Star, Distinguished Service Medal, Legion of Merit and a host of foreign honors.

Several biographies and military history works have been written detailing the life and campaigns of General Patton. However, his fame was assured for future generations by the highly popular 1970 movie, **Patton**, which faithfully documented his World War II experience. The movie and its star, George C. Scott ,won Academy Awards.

George C. Scott invades North Africa in the screen version of *Patton.* **(Credit: Film Favorites)**

Gen. Patton in Germany at war's end, 1945. (Credit: Film Favorites)

SIDNEY POITIER

He was born in Miami, Florida in 1924. His parents were poor Bahamans who had moved to Florida to be tomato growers. He returned to Nassau, the Bahama Islands for schooling but left before graduation and worked in various menial jobs before an underage enlistment in the U.S. Army.

Poitier was assigned to the 1267th Medical Group as a physiotherapist and stationed at Veterans Hospital, Long Island. He was honorably discharged in 1945.

Joining the American Negro Theatre for dramatic training, he made his stage debut on Broadway in the 1946 all-negro production of "Lysistrata", then toured with "Anna Lucasta". He then won a role in a 1950 U.S. Army Signal Corps documentary, "From Whom Cometh My Help".

He was an instant success in Hollywood becoming its number one black actor and breaking the old stereotype of blacks as previously portrayed on the screen. Poitier gave several moving performances early in his film career and won an Academy Award nomination for **The Defiant Ones** (1958) and took an Oscar for Best Actor in **Lilies of the Field** (1963).

Poitier has performed in fifty some films in his lifetime, some of the more notable being: **Cry the Beloved Country** (1952), **The Blackboard Jungle** (1955), **Porgy and Bess** (1959), **A Raisin in the Sun** (1961), **Duel at Diablo** (1966) , **To Sir With Love** and **Guess Whose Coming to Dinner** (1969), **They Call Me Mr. Tibbs** (1970) and **Deadly Pursuit** (1988).

He has also directed several movies in the 70s and 80s and entered the TV medium. His 1991 TV portrayal of Thurgood Marshall in "Separate But Equal" was highly acclaimed. In 1992 he became the first black entertainer to receive the American Film Institutes Life Achievement Award.

Poitier lives today with actress Joanna Shimkus his second wife.

TYRONE POWER

Born May 5, 1913 as Tyrone Edmund Power, Jr., in Cincinnati, Ohio, he was the son of a silent screen star and grandson of an Irish stage actor.

He started in show business in the early 1930's with some stage work and movie bit parts, his film debut being in 1932. With his dark good looks and

Sidney Poitier (right) as he appeared in the United Artists movie, *The Defiant Ones* with Tony Curtis. (Credit: Film Favorites)

Tyrone Power and Anne Baxter in a scene from 20th Century Fox's *Crash Dive*, Power's last film before entering military service. (Credit: Film Favorites)

acting ability he soon became a screen favorite and a box office success. He was in some two dozen films before his career was interrupted by the war. Some of the best were: **Suez** (1938), **Jesse James** (1939), **Johnny Apollo** (1940), **Son of Fury** (1942), **The Black Swan** (1942) and **Crash Dive** (1943).

Immediately after shooting **Crash Dive** Power enlisted in the Marine Corps and went through flying school, winning his wings and receiving a commission as second lieutenant in April 1943. He was assigned to a transport squadron, VMR-353 in the Marianas and flew a Curtiss C-46, twin-engine cargo plane in support of combat operations on Iwo Jima and later Okinawa.

Shipped home in 1945 he received an honorable discharge as captain in January 1946 and resumed his film making. His second postwar movie, **Nightmare Alley** in 1947, won him critical acclaim.

Power acted alternately on stage and in the movies. Some of his best remembered films are: **The Razor's Edge** (1946), **Captain From Castile** (1947), **Diplomatic Courier** (1952), **King of the Khyber Rifles** (1954), **The Long Gray Line** (1955), **The Eddie Duchin Story** (1956), **The Sun Also Rises** (1957) and **Witness for the Prosecution** (1958).

He was married three times and his two children Romaina and Tyrone Jr. are in the movies. He suffered a heart attack and died in Madrid in 1958 while filming **Solomon and Sheba**.

Lt. Tyrone Power, in his Marine Corps dress blues, delivers a speech at a bond rally, assisted by a Marine Corps band and a major general. (Credit: The Academy of Motion Picture Arts and Sciences)

ROBERT PRESTON

Born in 1918 in Newton Highlands, Massachusetts as Robert Preston Meservey, he was raised in Hollywood. Preston dropped out of school at age 16 and joined a Shakespearean company then put in a stint at the Pasadena Community Playhouse.

He won his first movie role in 1938, acting in a variety of roles, but without any leap to stardom.

Preston enlisted in the Army Air Force in 1943, and was trained as an intelligence officer. He was assigned to a combat unit in the Ninth Air Force in England and served there until war's end rising to the rank of captain.

He returned to movie making in 1947. However, his greatest fame was attained on the New York stage as Prof. Harold Hill in the smash hit musical, **The Music Man**, (1957). He won a Tony for that memorable performance then duplicated the award in 1966 with **I Do! I Do!. Music Man,** with Preston in his stage role, became a 1962 movie. He won an Academy Award nomination for his unique role in **Victoria/ Victoria** (1982).

Preston performed in some 45 films. Some of the more memorable were: **Beau Geste** (1939), **The Dark at the Top of the Stairs** (1960), **All the Way Home** (1963), **Mame** (1974) and **S.O.B.** (1981). His last screen role was in 1984, **The Last Starfighter.**

He died in 1987.

ERNIE PYLE

Born in Dana, Indiana as Ernest Taylor Pyle, on August 3, 1900, he became the most famous and widely read war correspondent of World War II.

He attended Indiana University, graduating in 1923 and got his first job as a cub reporter with the LaPorte (Indiana) Hearld. Pyle later worked for the Washington (D.C.) Daily News, the New York Evening World, the New York Evening Post and the Scripps-Howard newspapers. He was managing editor for the Washington Daily News from 1932 to 1935. Along the way he married Geraldine Siebolds, and gained fame as a crack journalist.

Robert Preston (right) gets cozy with Veronica Lake and Alan Ladd doesn't seem to like it, in this clip from *This Gun For Hire*. (Credit: Film Favorites)

The Scripps-Howard chain (over 200 newspapers) sent him to cover the war in Europe in 1941, and from that experience he wrote his first book, "Ernie Pyle In England". After the U.S. entered the war Pyle covered the conflict on battlefronts in North Africa, Italy and then Northern Europe after D-Day. He was a front line correspondent who earned the trust and admiration of common soldiers as he slogged through the war with them and lived under their harsh conditions. He published two more books, "Here is Your War" and "Brave Men", and won a Pulitzer Prize for distinguished correspondence in 1944.

As the war in Europe seemed to be winding down to its conclusion, Pyle felt obliged to observe and report on the Pacific battlefront. He made it to Iwo Jima and went ashore with the Okinawa invasion. A few days later he joined Army forces that had invaded Ie Shima Island, a small island within sight of Okinawa. It was the last invasion of the war, what troops in the Pacific called, "The Last Damned Island."

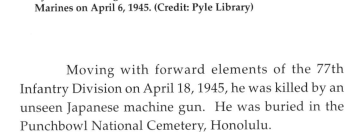

Pyle takes messages for the folks back home from Okinawa Marines on April 6, 1945. (Credit: Pyle Library)

Moving with forward elements of the 77th Infantry Division on April 18, 1945, he was killed by an unseen Japanese machine gun. He was buried in the Punchbowl National Cemetery, Honolulu.

Ernie Pyle aboard a U.S. Navy destroyer in the Pacific on 27 March 1945. (Credit: Pyle Library)

(Credit: Lambert Archives)

RONALD W. REAGAN

"The Great Communicator" as he became known during his political career, was born in Tampico, Illinois in 1911. His education was entirely in local public schools and he received his B.A. in economics and sociology from Eureka College, Illinois.

During his youth in the Midwest Reagan enrolled in a series of Army home-study extension courses which led him into the Enlisted Reserve. He was appointed a 2nd lieutenant in the Reserve Officers' Corps on May 25,1937 and was assigned to the 323rd Cavalry.

He made his Hollywood film debut in 1937 in **Love Is In The Air.** His portrayal of Frank Gipp in the 1940 **Knute Rockne - All American** propelled him to movie fame.

Reagan was ordered to active duty on April 19, 1942, but due to eyesight difficulties was classified for limited service. After assignments at the San Francisco Port of Embarkation, Fort Mason, the Air Force requested his services to produce training and propaganda films. He was also assigned to the show, **This is the Army**, by Irving Berlin. He was honorably

The 1937 movie was *Knute Rockne-All American* and starred Pat O'Brien (right) as the immortal Notre Dame coach. But the 26 year-old Ronald Reagan, as Frank Gipp, stole the show. From his dying words in the movie, came the oft repeated line, "Win one for the Gipper." (Credit: Film Favorites)

(Right) Made before the U.S. entered the war, Ronald Reagan starred in this movie about the British struggle. (Credit: Film Favorites)

(Below) Ronald Reagan appeared in Warner Bros.' *This is the Army*, a popular wartime musical by Irving Berlin. (Credit: Film Favorites)

Ronald Reagan (left) and Errol Flynn (center right) hope to confuse the Nazis in this Warner Bros. movie, *Desperate Journey.* (Credit: Film Favorites)

Capt. Ronald Reagan, U.S. Army in World War II. (Credit: Academy of Motion Picture Arts and Sciences)

separated from active duty in December 1945 with the rank of Captain.

Reagan was elected to the presidency of the Screen Actors' Guild by his peers and served in that role from 1947 to 1952.

He had many postwar film credits including **The Killers** (1946), **Prisoner of War** (1957), and **Hellcats of the Navy** (1957).

In the mid-1960s Reagan began his career in politics. He served as Governor of California from 1966 to 1974. After that tour in office he began to be a very vocal and articulate champion for conservative causes.

Nominated by the Republican Party, he won the Presidency of the United States and was inaugurated in 1981. President Reagan served two terms in office.

He resides in retirement in California at this writing.

A pair of future baseball Hall of Famers get together for a game in Hawaii. Joe DiMaggio (left) played for a Seventh Air Force team and Pee Wee Reese (second from the right) was with the Navy Hospital at Aeia Heights. They seem to be signing baseballs for the two staff officers. (Credit: National Baseball Museum, Cooperstown, NY)

PEE WEE REESE

Born Harold H. Reese in 1918 at Akron, Kentucky, he became of baseball's outstanding shortstops of all time.

Dubbed "Pee Wee" by his teammates after joining the Brooklyn Dodgers in 1940, he became an instant hit with the Brooklyn faithful.

In 1942 he joined military service and was assigned to a Navy special service unit. He was honorably discharged in 1945 and returned to the Dodgers the next season.

Reese was still with the Dodger organization when they made the cross-country move to Los Angeles. He played for 16 years for just one team and had a .269 lifetime batting average. He was in seven World Series and was elected to the Baseball Hall of Fame in 1984.

JASON ROBARDS

Robards was born in Chicago, Illinois in 1922. His family moved to California and he attended Hollywood High School. He studied at the Academy of Dramatic Arts in New York and it was there that his acting career began while Robards worked at odd jobs.

He enlisted in the U.S. Navy in 1940 and was stationed at Pearl Harbor as an enlisted radio operator when the Japanese attacked on December 7, 1941. He went on to participate in thirteen naval engagements in the Pacific. His ships were twice torpedoed and he received the Navy Cross for conspicuous valor. Later in the war he served on the staff of Admiral Raymond Spruance.

Returning to Broadway, he labored in relative obscurity until winning praise for his role in Eugene O'Neill's 1956 drama, "The Iceman Cometh." In 1957 he won the New York Drama Critics' Award for his performance in "Long Day's Journey Into Night."

Jason Robards (Credit: The Academy of Motion Picture Arts and Sciences)

It was not until 1959 that he made his first movie, **The Journey,** and he alternated between stage and screen. He received the Best Supporting Actor Oscar for **All the President's Men** in 1976 and another for **Julia** in 1977.

Some of his other film credits are: **A Thousand Clowns, Divorce American Style, Hour of the Gun, Tora! Tora! Tora!, Melvin and Howard, Something Wicked This Way Comes,** and **Philadelphia.**

JACKIE ROBINSON

Born of an impoverished sharecropper family in Cairo, Georgia in 1919, Jack Roosevelt Robinson became one of America's most celebrated athletes.

His father abandoned the family and Robinson's mother moved her five children to Pasadena, California. Jackie starred in several sports in high school, at Pasadena Junior College and at UCLA.

Financial considerations forced him to leave UCLA before graduation and he entered the U.S. Army in 1942.

After attending officer candidate school he was commissioned a second lieutenant in 1943 and assigned to a segregated black quartermaster unit. Robinson's opposition to what he believed to be racial discrimination led to his court martial for insubordination. He was subsequently acquitted and granted an honorable discharge.

In 1945 he won a berth at second base with the Kansas City Monarchs of the Negro League. His athletic talent and fiercely competitive style brought him to the attention of a major league scout for the Brooklyn Dodgers General Manager, Branch Rickey. A brilliant administrator and an enlightened individual, Rickey integrated major league baseball through the adept introduction and handling of Robinson. Opposed by many baseball owners and players, Jackie broke into the big leagues in 1947, the first Negro to do so.

Displaying indomitable courage and extraordinary class in the face of bigotry, he proved to be a standout as a fielder, batter and base runner and won the acclaim of fans and the respect of fellow players. In ten years with the Dodgers he compiled a

Jackie Robinson at old Ebbets Field, Brooklyn. (Credit: National Baseball Library, Cooperstown, NY)

batting average of .311, stole 197 bases, drove in 734 runs and was involved in six National League pennant races.

In 1962 he was elected to the Baseball Hall of Fame.

He retired to business as a vice-president for Chock Full o' Nuts Company where he continued to be an activist in the cause of civil rights. He died of heart disease in 1972 leaving his widow, Rachel Isum, whom he had married in 1954, and two surviving children.

MICKEY ROONEY

The son of vaudevillians, "Mickey" was born Joe Yule, Jr. on September 23, 1920 in Brooklyn. He made his first stage appearance before he was two and was part of the family stage act. He made his first film appearance as a midget in **Not to Be Trusted** (1926), a six year old.

He then gained fame with young and old in some 50 two-reel comedies, titled **Mickey Maguire**, shot between 1927 and 1933. But his greatest popularity was spawned by a series of 15 films in which he played "Andy Hardy", the son of a small town judge. These sentimental comedies appeared on screen between 1937

Mickey Rooney (center), strapped into parachute harness, seems ready for a hop in this Ninth Air Force P-61 Black Widow, of the 422nd Night Fighter Squadron in Europe in 1945. (Credit: Campbell Archives)

Mickey Rooney (seated left) starred in this Blake Edwards story for Columbia Pictures, *All Ashore*. (Credit: Film Favorites)

Mickey Rooney tries to cope with his Japanese captors in this scene from the war movie, *Ambush Bay*. (Credit: Film Favorites)

Mickey Rooney (right) and William Holden battle it out with the North Koreans in a scene from *The Bridges at Toko-Ri*. (Credit: Film Favorites)

and 1947 - a sample title, **Andy Hardy Meets Debutante**. And while the Hardy series was slightly corny, Rooney interspersed several dramatic roles during the same period: **The Adventures of Huckleberry Finn** (1939), **Men of Boys Town** (1941), **The Human Comedy** (1943) and **National Velvet** (1944).

When he reached draft age in 1943, Rooney went into the Army and was assigned to an entertainment unit. He saw most of his service in Europe until honorably discharged in 1946.

Returning to his movie career he acted in a variety of rolls, but no longer the buoyant teenager. Some of his dramatic finest were: **The Bridges at Toko-Ri** (1955), a Korean war story; **The Bold and the Brave** (1956), and **Baby Face Nelson** (1957).

Despite his entertainment fame Rooney could not escape problems of the heart and the wallet. He was married and divorced seven times before settling into wedded bliss. And in 1962 he declared bankruptcy, much of his trouble coming from alimony demands.

His movie roles became less than classic, i.e. **How to Stuff a Wild Bikini** (1965) and **Pete's Dragon** (1977). Yet he persevered in both the film and stage medium. He won an Oscar for Best Supporting Actor for **Black Stallion** in 1979 and won an Emmy for his 1982 portrayal of a retarded man in the made for TV movie, **Bill**.

Rooney had sensational success on Broadway in 1979 with "Sugar Babies", toured with that show, and returned to Broadway for "The Will Rogers Follies." His latest movies are **The Legend of Wolf Mountain** and **Little Nemo** (1992)

ARCHIBALD ROOSEVELT

Born in 1894, "Archie" was the youngest of President Teddy Roosevelt's children. He graduated from Harvard University in 1917 and immediately entered the U.S. Army.

In France with the A.E.F. he was decorated, wounded and gassed before being invalided back home.

Between the World Wars he became an investment banker and steered away from politics.

ELLIOTT ROOSEVELT

Born in 1910 to Franklin Delano and Eleanor Roosevelt, he refused to attend Harvard in the family tradition but went into advertising and radio. Elliott was commissioned a captain in the Army Air Corps in 1941.

Though not a pilot he became an expert in photo reconnaissance and flew on some seventy-five missions over Europe, winning the Distinguished Flying Cross and Air Medal. Franklin rose to command the 3rd Reconnaissance Group in the Mediterranean theatre of war, and later the multi-national 325th Photo Reconnaissance Wing. He retired from the Air Force after the war having achieved the temporary rank of brigadier general. His other awards included the Legion of Merit, Britain's Order of the British Empire and the French Croix de Guerre.

Some degree of controversy attended Elliott's military service. His final rank was thought to be excessive by pilots who had seen as much or more combat. An incident wherein he brought his dog aboard

Col. Archibald Roosevelt in New Guinea in 1943. (Credit: Theodore Roosevelt Collection, Harvard College Library)

At the outbreak of World War II he again offered his services and campaigned in the Southwest Pacific with the United States Army 41st Infantry Division. During battles in New Guinea and Biak he was wounded by shrapnel and again invalided out of active service. He retired from the Army with the rank of colonel and returned to the investment banking business. Colonel Roosevelt retired to Florida and died there in 1979.

His decorations included the Silver Star and three oak leaf clusters, the Bronze Star Medal, the Purple Heart with one cluster, the French Croix de Guerre and several other foreign honors.

Col. Elliott Roosevelt (left) at the Casablanca Conference in January 1943. To the right is his younger brother Lt. John Roosevelt. (Credit: USAF via Franklin D. Roosevelt Library)

an Air Force transport causing an enlisted man to be bumped made the newspapers, although Elliott said he was unaware of the bumping. He was also involved with Howard Hughes development of an aircraft that was purchased by the Air Force, and their was open criticism of some wining and dining by Hughes associates. Elliott met the third of his five wives, Faye Emerson, through the Hughes connection.

After the war he became a radio and TV producer, moved to Florida to try his hand at politics and was elected to the office of Mayor of Miami Beach in 1965 but was not reelected. He later moved to the Southwest where he owned an oil and gas firm.

He wrote several history books including a three volume work entitled, **The Roosevelts of Hyde Park** and **As He Saw It**.

He died in 1990 in Scottsdale, Arizona.

FRANKLIN D. ROOSEVELT, JR.

Namesake and son of the 32nd President of the United States, he was born in 1914.

Franklin joined the United States Navy prior to the U.S. entry into World War II and served on destroyers and destroyer-escorts in virtually every theatre of war.

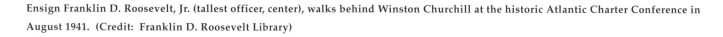

Ensign Franklin D. Roosevelt, Jr. (tallest officer, center), walks behind Winston Churchill at the historic Atlantic Charter Conference in August 1941. (Credit: Franklin D. Roosevelt Library)

JAMES ROOSEVELT

He won the Silver Star for gallantry in action and the Purple Heart for wounds received during the invasion of Sicily in August 1943 when as a lieutenant his ship, Destroyer *Mayrant* was damaged in Palermo harbor by German bombers.

Later in the war, as a Lieutenant Commander he skippered Destroyer-Escort *Ulvert M. Moore* in the invasion of the Philippines and the invasion of Okinawa and was awarded the Legion of Merit.

Elected to the U.S. House of Representative from New York in 1949, Franklin later served in the John Kennedy administration as an Under Secretary of Commerce and was appointed to the Equal Opportunity Commission by President Lyndon Johnson.

His political and government involvement ended with a failed bid for the governorship of New York in 1966. He then involved himself in business and owned a Fiat car dealership. He died in 1988.

The eldest son of President Franklin D. Roosevelt and Eleanor, "Jimmy" was educated at Harvard and served in his father's early administration.

With the advent of World War II he joined the United States Marine Corps and completed officers candidate school. Assigned to Col. Edson Carlson's Raider Battalion, Roosevelt participated in the August 1942 raid on Makin Island in the Gilberts. A major at the time and second in command of the battalion, Roosevelt so distinguished himself in this action that he was awarded the Navy Cross (second only to the Medal of Honor) for his valor and the rescue of fellow Marines.

Later in the war he participated in combat on Guadalcanal, Tarawa and the invasion of Makin where he won the Silver Star for gallantry. He attained the rank of lieutenant colonel.

After the war he tried his hand at politics, being elected to the House of Representatives in 1954 and then defeated in a run for the mayoral office of Los Angeles in 1965. He served for a time in the United Nations. He died in 1991.

Lt. Col. Jimmy Roosevelt (center, wearing glasses) during the Makin Island raid of August 1942. (Credit: U.S. Navy via Franklin D. Roosevelt Library)

JOHN A. ROOSEVELT

Born in 1916, John was the youngest son of President Franklin D. and Eleanor Roosevelt. He attended Groton and Harvard, graduating in 1938.

He joined the U.S. Navy at the outbreak of World War II and was assigned to the Navy Supply Corps. He got sea duty after pleading with his father for a combat role. As a lieutenant commander he won the Bronze Star for actions while his aircraft carrier, the U.S.S. *Wasp* was under attack in the Pacific.

Except for a brief flirtaion with the 1957 New York City mayoral race, Roosevelt did not seek political office, as did his brothers. He openly supported Republican Dwight Eisenhower in th 1952 presidential election.

He spent his postwar life largely as an investment banker and died in 1981.

Lt. John Roosevelt, in late 1943. (Credit: Boris, Boston, via Franklin D. Roosevelt Library)

KERMIT ROOSEVELT

Born in 1889 to President Teddy Roosevelt and wife Edith, Kermit was educated at Harvard University.

He joined the British Army prior to U.S. entry in World War I. Rising to the rank of captain, he won the Military Cross for valor while serving in Mesopotamia. After the United States declared war on Germany he transferred to the U.S. Army, served in France with the 7th Field Artillery, 1st Infantry Division, and was discharged in 1918.

He formed the Roosevelt Steamship Compay and with other business associates organized United States Lines.

In 1939 he rejoined the British Army and sought to raise a contingent of volunteers to serve with Finland in its war with Russia. However, the Finns negotiated a peace treaty before the regiment could be employed. A major with the Middlesex Regiment he fought in campaigns in Norway and the Middle East.

After America's entry in World War II he transferred to the U.S. Army despite questions about his health and ability to serve. Kermit was assigned as an intelligence officer and flew on aerial missions against Japanese bases in the Aleutian Islands. Despondent over his health and inability to engage in combat, he commited suicide while on active service, June 3, 1943 and is buried at Fort Richardson, Alaska.

Editor's Note:
No photo was available of Kermit Roosevelt, but it was felt that his absence in this work would be an injustice. Likewise there are no photos nor any biographies of President Theodore Roosevelt's four grandsons, all of whom served in uniform in World War II.

The youngest child of President Theodore Roosevelt, Quentin, joined the U.S. Army Air Service in World War I. He flew a fighter plane in France and was shot down and killed in 1918 at the age of 21. Hence, every male child of Presidents Theodore and Franklin Roosevelt served in uniform and saw combat.

THEODORE ROOSEVELT, JR.

Born in 1887 "Ted" was the first son of President Theodore Roosevelt. He soldiered in France in World War I where he was gassed, wounded and decorated while serving with the 26th Infantry Regiment, 1st Infantry Division.

Between the wars he was instrumental in founding the American Legion and served as an assistant secretary of the Navy from 1921 to 1924. He later became a vice president of the Doubleday, Doran publishing firm and between the World Wars wrote or co-authored several volumes on history and travel.

Anticipating another war, he sought active duty and was assigned to his old regiment in April 1941. He led elements of the 1st Infantry Division ashore in the November 1942 invasion near Oran. During North African fighting he became renowned for his courage.

Transferred to England in anticipation of the Second Front, Teddy was promoted to brigadier general and appointed deputy commander of the 4th Infantry Division.

Col. Ted Roosevelt, Jr. in 1942 as his regiment trained for combat in North Africa. At the right is his son Quentin Roosevelt, II, who also served with the regiment in action. (Credit: Theodore Roosevelt Collection, Harvard College Library)

During the invasion of Normandy, June 6, 1944, he was in the first boat to hit shore at Utah Beach with elements of the 8th Infantry Regiment. The highest ranking officer on the beachhead for much of D-Day, he inspired troops with his coolness under fire.

Although walking with a cane and suffering from a heart ailment he had not disclosed to medical personnel, he continued to stay in the front lines.

On July 12, 1944 while battling through the Normandy hedgerows he suffered a fatal heart attack at age 57. Teddy died unaware that he had just been appointed a division commander.

For his repeated acts of leadership and displays of courage in Normandy he was given a posthumous award of the Medal of Honor, America's highest combat decoration. During two wars he had also accumulated the Distinguished Service Cross (second only to the Medal of Honor), the Distinguished Service Medal,

Col. Theodore "Ted" Roosevelt, Jr. in 1941 on his return to the Army. (Credit: Theodore Roosevelt Collection, Harvard College Library)

Brig. Gen. Ted Roosevelt, Jr. in France, 1944 with the 4th Division. (Credit: Theodore Roosevelt Collection, Harvard College Library)

Purple Heart, Silver Star with three clusters, the Legion of Honor, the Croix de Guerre with three palms from France, the Croix de Guerre with palms from Belgium, and several other foreign decorations.

DAN ROWAN

Born in 1922 in Beggs, Oklahoma as Daniel H. David, his parents were carnival workers. Orphaned in childhood, he grew up at the McClelland Home in Pueblo, Colorado. By the time he reached high school he had become a two letter athlete, worked on the yearbook and was class president. In 1940 he went to Hollywood hoping for a career in movies and worked around the perifery as a handy man.

When World War II started he joined the Army Air Force and won his wings and commission as a second lieutenant. After advanced training in fighters he received orders sending him to the Southwest Pacific.

Assigned to the 8th Fighter Squadron, 49th Fighter Group, Fifth Air Force in New Guinea, he flew a Curtiss P-40 fighter plane. On September 21, 1943 he downed two enemy aircraft in an air battle. He was later shot down himself but survived to complete his combat tour, returned to the States and was honorably discharged in 1945.

Returning to Los Angeles, he took acting courses at UCLA and USC. In 1952 he met Dick Martin, then a bartender, and the two concocted a night club comedy act. The act had only moderate success in local clubs but led to a movie **Once Upon a Horse** in 1958. There was a TV spot on "The Ed Sullivan Show" in 1960 and then a successful comedy record album. In between these modest successes nightclub acts were their bread and butter.

Asked to fill in for a vacationing Dean Martin on his NBC-TV variety show in 1966, the Rowan-Martin duo earned the highest ratings of any show that summer, and with that boost the concept of their NBC comedy-variety act series was hatched. Thus the zany, irreverent "Laugh In" was born. It showed regularly from 1968 to 1972 and won four Emmys. As an offshoot of the TV show they made another comedy film, **The Maltese Bippy**, in 1969.

Dan Rowan died in 1987.

Dan Rowan rests on his P-40 fighter in China. (Credit: Sammy Pierce via Ernie McDowell)

DARRELL ROYAL

Born in Hollis, Oklahoma in 1924, he was a natural athlete in high school.

Inducted into the Army in 1943 he attended gunnery school but was assigned to a special service unit because of his athletic ability. Stationed at Will Rogers Field he was a physical education instructor until his discharge in 1946.

After the war he entered the University of Oklahoma and tried out for the football team. Although he was one of the smallest at 168 pounds, he made the team with his skill and determination. He played quarterback, halfback, defensive back, punter and punt returner and played on the 1946-49 teams. He became an all-American on these championship teams.

After his playing days he had a successful coaching career that spanned twenty years with the University of Texas. His record was 167 wins, 47 losses and five ties, and his Longhorn teams won eleven Southwest Conference football crowns. He retired from active coaching in 1977 and from the University of Texas Athletic Director post in 1980. However, he is still active in University affairs.

ROBERT RYAN

Born in Chicago, Illinois in 1909, he was educated at Loyola Academy, Chicago, and Dartmouth. A college boxer and man of considerable physical stature, and good looks, Ryan worked at a variety of tasks until arriving at acting in 1939. He first worked on Broadway then went to the film capital in 1940. He was in twelve movies before World War II.

Darrell Royal in his gridiron glory days. (Credit: Darrell Royal)

A movie poster for *Flying Leathernecks* highlights the stars, Robert Ryan (left), John Wayne and Janis Carter. (Credit: Film Favorites)

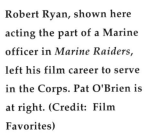

Robert Ryan, shown here acting the part of a Marine officer in *Marine Raiders*, left his film career to serve in the Corps. Pat O'Brien is at right. (Credit: Film Favorites)

Enlisting in the Marine Corps in 1943, he was trained as a drill instructor and served in that capacity at Camp Pendleton, California until receiving his honorable discharge in 1945.

He returned to Hollywood and took on a variety of film roles while also keeping his hand in the theatre. Some of his memorable performances were in the following movies: **Crossfire** (1947), **Act of Violence** (1948), **Clash by Night** (1952), **Inferno** (1953), **Bad Day at Black Rock** (1955), **God's Little Acre** (1958), **King of Kings** (1958), **Billy Budd** and **The Longest Day** (1962), **The Dirty Dozen** (1967), **The Wild Bunch** (1969), **The Iceman Cometh** (1973) and his last, **The Outfit** (1974).

Ryan was active in civic matters and was a founder of UCLA Theatre Group and a school in the San Fernando Valley of California. He died of cancer in 1973.

Robert Ryan in a scene from the movie, *Escape to Burma*. (Credit: Film Favorites)

SABU

Born in Mysore, India in 1924 as Sabu Dastagir, he was working as a stable boy for an Indian maharajah when discovered by British movie mogul Robert Flaherty. His first film was **Elephant Boy** in 1937.

Working for the film industry in both England and Hollywood, Sabu was used in a series of exotic foreign epics such as **Drums** (1938), **The Thief of Baghdad** (1940) and **Arabian Nights** (1942).

Having achieved U.S. citizenship he enlisted in the Army Air Force in 1944 and was assigned as a gunner on a B-24 Liberator with the 308th Bomb Group based in China. He flew 42 missions winning the Distinguished Flying Cross and the Air Medal with four Oak Leaf Clusters.

Postwar interest in Middle East adventure films had faded in Hollywood and Sabu made most of his remaining films in Europe.

A few of the more notable of his later movies are: **Black Narcissus** (1947), **Man Eater of Kumaon**

Sabu appears as a young man in this still from the movie, *Jungle Book*, adapted from Rudyard Kipling's book of the same name. (Credit: Film Favorites)

(1948), **Savage Drums** (1951), **Rampage** (1963) and his last, **A Tiger Walks** (1964).

He died of a heart attack in 1963 at the age of thirty-nine.

Sabu in China between the twin .50 caliber machine guns of the ball turret of his B-24 bomber. (Credit: Academy of Motion Picture Arts and Sciences)

GEORGE C. SCOTT

Born George Campbell Scott in Wise, Virginia in 1926, he grew up in Detroit.

He was educated at the University of Missouri, School of Journalism and had his first acting experience with the campus drama group.

Enlisting in the U.S. Marine Crops in 1945 he expected to see combat in the Pacific but the war ended too soon and he spent his enlistment as a creative writing instructor and a member of the Arlington National Cemetery burial unit.

After work in summer stock and some off-Broadway theatre he made it to Broadway and was in a television series, "East Side, West Side," before tackling Hollywood. He first appeared in films in 1959 and immediately made an impression with his dynamic presence, and intense style. He won an Academy Award (which he refused to accept) in 1971 for **Patton** and an Emmy for his work in the TV play, "The Price", a prize he also rejected.

Some of his best movies are: **Anatomy of a Murder** (1959), **The Hustler** (1961), **Dr. Strangelove** (1964), **The Flim-Flam Man** (1976), **The New Centurions** (1972), **The Day of the Dolphin** (1973), **Islands in the Stream** (1977), **Taps** (1981), **The Exorcist III** (1990) and **Malice** (1993).

George C. Scott in his 1971 Academy Award winning portrayal of General Patton. (Credit: Film Favorites)

George C. Scott as a deranged general in Columbia's 1964 anti-war hit, *Dr. Strangelove*. (Credit: Film Favorites)

His success in made-for-television movies has also been impressive. He has appeared in that medium in "Oliver", as Scrooge in "A Christmas Carol", "Mussolini: The Untold Story" and a series, "Mr. President."

He has been married five time and has five children.

ROBERT SCOTT

Born in Macon, Georgia as Robert Lee Scott, Jr. in 1908, he graduated from the U.S. Military Academy at West Point in 1932.

After taking flight training he became an aviator and a fighter pilot.

Shortly after World War II began he was dispatched to China and arrived in the summer of 1942 as Chennault's American Volunteer Group was being disbanded. Only a handful of the AVG pilots and ground crews elected to join the surviving 23rd Fighter Group of the U.S. Fourteenth Air Force, and Colonel Scott took command of that under strength unit. Fighting against superior Japanese air forces, Scott led his unit to considerable success over the balance of 1942.

Col. Robert L. Scott in the cockpit of a P-40 like the one he flew in China to become an ace. (Credit: Lambert Archives)

Brig. Gen. Robert L. Scott, author, warrior. (Credit: USAF)

He personally accounted for twelve enemy aircraft and was decorated with the Silver Star and One Oak Leaf Cluster, the Distinguished Flying Cross and two Clusters, the British D.F.C. and several Chinese decorations.

Returning to stateside assignments he received his M.S. at the National War College and retired as a brigadier general in 1957. He has lectured widely and written several books: "God is My Co-Pilot" (1943) which was made into a movie, "Damned to Glory" (1944), "Runway to the Sun" (1945), "Between the Elephant's Eyes" (1954), "Look of the Eagle" (1955), "Samburu" (1957), "Tiger in the Sky" (1959), "Flying Tiger: Chennault of China" (1959), and "Boring a Hole in the Sky" (1961).

Enos "Country" Slaughter. (Credit: National Baseball Library, Cooperstown, NY)

ENOS SLAUGHTER

Born in 1916 in Roxboro, North Carolina, "Country" Slaughter was one of major league baseballs most firecely competetive players.

He joined the St. Louis Cardinals in 1938 as an outfielder and played until 1942 when he was called to the colors.

Slaughter served in the Army Air Force from 1943 until 1945 in non-combat duties.

Returning to the Cards, he played from 1946 until 1953 and was a factor in several pennant races and World Series. He was traded to the American League in 1954, playing with the Yankees and then Kansas City until 1959.

He retired from baseball in 1960 with a lifetime batting average of .300 and 169 homeruns. He played in five World Series and was inducted into the Baseball Hall of Fame in 1985.

DEKE SLAYTON

One of the original Mercury astronauts, he was born March 1, 1924 in Sparta, Wisconsin as Donald K. Slayton.

He entered the Army Aviation Cadet program and received his wings and commission as a second lieutenant in April 1943. After advanced training he was assigned to the 340th Bomb Group and flew 56 combat missions in the Mediterranean Theatre of Operations as pilot of a B-25 Mitchell. He was rotated back to the States in 1944 but volunteered for another combat tour and went to Okinawa in April 1945 with the 319th Bomb Group. Flying the A-26 Invader he logged another seven combat missions over Japan.

He left the Air Force long enough to attain a degree in aeronautical engineering from the University of Minnesota in 1949, then was recalled to active duty in 1951 during the Korean crisis. He had duty assignments in various U.S. locations and in Bitburg, Germany. He later attended the USAF Test Pilot School at Edwards AFB, California and was stationed at Edwards from 1956 to 1959 participating in a number of test programs. He attained the rank of Major.

In 1959 "Deke" was named as one of the seven original Mercury astronauts but was relieved of this assignment due to a heart condition that was diagnosed in August 1959. He stayed with NASA in various roles until being reinstated to flight status in 1972.

The seven original Mercury astronauts: Left to right Scott Carpenter, Gordon Cooper, John Glenn, Virgil Grissom, Walter Schirra, Alan Shepard, and Deke Slayton. (Credit: NASA)

Deke Slayton, astronaut. (Credit: NASA)

Dr. Slayton made his first space flight in July 1975 as Apollo docking module pilot for the joint U.S.-Russian flight culminating in the first meeting in space of orbital craft. Returning to NASA he served as manager for orbital flight tests and was responsible for the 747/Orbiter ferry program.

In addition to a number of combat decorations he has received honorary degrees in science and engineering from Carthage College, Illinois and Michigan Technological University, Houghton,

Editor's Note:
Of the seven original astronauts, only Glenn and Slayton saw significant action in WW II. Alan Shepard graduated from the Naval Academy in 1944 and saw limited Pacific service on the destroyer **Cogwell**. *Gordon Cooper was an enlisted man in the Marine Corps in 1945. Wally Schirra graduated from the Naval Academy in 1945 and went to flight training. Scott Carpenter and Virgil Grisson entered military service some years after the war.*

ROBERT STACK

Born in Los Angeles in 1919, he was educated at the University of Southern California.

The handsome young actor appeared in his first movie, **First Love**, in 1939 and mostly played the youthful romantic through 1942.

Enlisting in the Navy, he completed officer training and served as a gunnery officer for three years. He was honorably discharged in 1946.

Returning to acting he won acclaim but no prize for his performances in **The Bull Fighter and the Lady** (1951) and **The High and the Mighty** (1954) and was nominated for best supporting actor for **Written on the Wind** in 1957. He has acted in some 40 films in the U.S., France, Italy, and Germany. Some of his other movies are: **Good Morning Miss Dove** (1955), **John Paul Jones** (1959), **The Caretakers** (1963), **Story of a Woman** (1969), **Airplane** (1980) and **Joe Versus the Volcano** (1990).

However, Stack's most consistent work and most public recognition was in television with his

Robert Stack in one of his early movies, *Eagle Squadron.* **(Credit: Film Favorites)**

portrayal of Elliot Ness in the series "The Untouchables" which ran from 1959-63. He won an Emmy for his work there in 1960. He also participated in the the 1968-71 series "Name of the Game"; the 1976-77 series "Most Wanted"; "Strike Force" in 1981-82 and "Unsolved Mysteries" which began in 1991 and continues at this writing.

In a good post war flying film, *Fighter Squadron* **by Warner Bros., Robert Stack had one of the lead roles. (Credit: Film Favorites)**

ROD STEIGER

Born in 1925 in Westhampton, New York, he quit school at 16, and lied about his age to join the U.S. Navy.

He served on the destroyer *Taussig* as a torpedoman in the South Pacific and through the invasions of Iwo Jima and Okinawa. He received an honorable discharge in August 1945.

Steiger worked with an amateur theatre group, then used his GI Bill of Rights at the Dramatic Workshop of New School for Social Research. Studying with two more New York dramatic groups he spent most of the 1950s on the New York Stage.

He was in the 1951 movie **Teresa** and did not return to Hollywood until 1954 when he starred opposite Marlon Brando in **On the Waterfront**, a role that won him a Best Supporting Actor nomination. He worked almost exclusively in pictures from then on, scoring another Oscar nomination in 1965 for **The Pawnbroker** and winning the Oscar for Best Actor in 1967 for **In the Heat of the Night**.

The consummate character actor, he has played Napoleon, Mussolini and Al Capone with believable recreations of each. He has appeared in over 60 movies made in the U.S., England, Italy, and Yugoslavia. Some of his other most memorable films are: **The Court Martial of Billy Mitchell** (1955), **Al Capone** (1959), **Doctor Shivago** (1965), **Waterloo** (1970), **Last Days of Mussolini** (1974), **The Amityville Horror** (1979), **The Chosen** (1981) and **Guilty as Charged** 1991.

Rod Steiger in a scene from *The Sergeant*. (Credit: Film Favorites)

JIMMY STEWART

James Stewart was born in 1908 in Indiana, Pennsylvania. He graduated from Princeton with a degree in architecture, but having performed in amateur productions before and during college he was easily influenced into a 1932 show at the University Playhouse in Falmouth, Massachusetts, where he became friends with Henry Fonda and Margaret Sullavan.

The lure of the footlights led him to Broadway and then to Hollywood where he appeared in his first film in 1935. Stewart's charm was in his shy, hesitant manner, the exact opposite of the classic Hollywood leading man. He was an early hit in **You Can't Take it With You** (1938), **It's a Wonderful Life** and **Mr. Smith Goes to Washington** (1939) and **The Philadelphia Story** (1940). He won the New York Film Critics Award for the first three and an Oscar for the last. With his career at a zenith he made just three more films then he enlisted in the Army Air Corps.

A flying buff, Stewart had logged over 400 hours when he got into the aviation cadet program. He won his wings and commission and was made an instructor for a period then placed in command of the 703rd Bomb Squadron in England flying B-24 Liberators. He was later assigned as Operations officer in the 453rd Bomb Group and subsequently went to the staff of an Eighth Air Force wing. Stewart completed

Aviation Cadet, Jimmy Stewart in a trainer. (Credit: Campbell Archives)

134

Maj. Jimmy Stewart is decorated with the Distinguished Flying Cross. (Credit: Campbell Archives)

twenty combat missions leading many himself and was a lieutenant colonel when the war ended. He was awarded the Distinguished Flying Cross, Air Medal with Oak Leaf Clusters, and the French Croix de Guerre.

Maj. Jimmy Stewart (seated) interrogates 453rd Bomb Group air crews after their mission over enemy territory. (Credit: USAF)

The 1954 film memorializing the life of Glenn Miller had Jimmy Stewart in the title role. (Credit: Film Favorites)

(Below) Lt. Gen. Valin, Chief of Staff of the French Air Force, awards the Croix de Guerre with Palm to Lt. Col. Jimmy Stewart. (Credit: USAF)

After the war he stayed in the Air Force Reserve and rose to the rank of brigadier general in 1959. He retired in 1968.

The intense combat of Stewart's service stint did not dull his acting ability nor did it dampen the enthusiasm of his movie fans. He won New York Film Critics Awards in 1959 for **Anatomy of a Murder.** He also won an Academy Award nomination for that film as well as **Harvey,** the classic comedy about a lovable loony. Some of his other memorable roles of his more than 80 films are: **Destry Rides Again** (1939), **Call Northside 777** (1948), **The Stratton Story** (1949), **Broken Arrow** (1950), **Bend of the River** (1952), **The Naked**

Jimmy Stewart (right) in a scene from *Flight of the Phoenix*. (Credit: Film Favorites)

Spur (1953), **The Glenn Miller Story** and **Rear Window** (1954), **The Spirit of St. Louis** (1957), **Vertigo** and **Bell Book and Candle** (1958), **The Man Who Shot Liberty Valance** (1962), **Shanendoah** (1965), **The Flight of the Phoenix** (1966), and **Cheyenne Social Club** (1970).

Stewart brought "Harvey" to Broadway in 1972 and worked in television with "The James Stewart Show (1971-72) and the drama series "Hawkins" (1973-74).

He received the American Film Institutes Lifetime Achievement Award in 1980, a similar honor by the Kenedy Center in 1983 and by the Film Society of Lincoln Center in 1990. He was given a special Oscar by the Academy in 1985.

In 1989 he produced a book of poetry. He has made no films in the 90s, but his voice was heard in an animated childrens' tale, **Fievel Goes West**, in 1991. He lives quietly enjoying his four children and several grandchildren. Gloria, his wife of 46 years died in 1994.

In a post war salute to LeMay's deterrent bombers, *Strategic Air Command*, Jimmy Stewart had the lead opposite June Allyson. (Credit: Film Favorites)

JOE STYDAHAR

Born in 1912 in Kaylor, Pennsylvania, and educated at the University of West Virginia, Joe was one of the all time standout line men in the National Football League.

He was the Chicago Bears number one choice in the first-ever NFL draft in 1936 and was a 60-minute performer who bulwarked the Bear's line during the famous "Monsters of the Midway" era. A huge player by 1930s standards (6 foot 4 inches - 230 pounds) he had incredible power and amazing speed for his size. He wore number 13, flaunting superstition, and shunned the use of a helmet until NFL rules forced him to comply. He was left tackle on the all-NFL team from 1937 to 1940.

At the outbreak of World War II he enlisted in the Navy and did not play service football but served for three years until his honorable discharge.

Returning to the Bears he played for two more years. During his tenure with the George Halas organization they won five Western Division titles and three NFL championships.

After his playing days Stydahar coached for the Los Angeles Rams between 1950-52 and for the St. Louis

Joe Stydahar (Credit: Chicago Bears Archives)

Cardinals 1953-54. He was inducted into the Pro Football Hall of Fame in 1967 and died in 1977.

ROBERT TAYLOR

One of the most recognizable profiles in Hollywood history was born in Filley, Nebraska in 1911 as Spangler Arlington Brugh. He attended Doan College in Crete, Nebraska and Pomona College in California.

Robert Taylor became a Navy pilot in the movies before the war in *Flight Command*. (Credit: Film Favorites)

138

With the screen name of Robert Taylor he made his film debut in 1934, in **Handy Andy** and there after became the quintessential "handsome leading man." He made 37 films in the years before he entered military service.

He enlisted the Navy flight training program in 1943, won his wings and commission as an ensign. His wife, Barbara Stanwyck, a star leading lady, attended the graduation ceremony.

Taylor was assigned as an instructor at the New Orleans Naval Air Station, but he also donated his time to war bond rallies and was involved in making training films. One of those films, an instructional piece on the N2S Stearman, is available today on VHS.

He left the service after the war with the rank of lieutenant, but continued his Navy association as narrator for the World War II Pacific documentary, **Fighting Lady** (1950).

Taylor made nearly 40 postwar movies including those made in England, Italy, France and Spain. Some of his films are: **Magnificent Obsession** (1935), **Camille** (1937), **A Yank at Oxford** (1938), **Johnny Eager** (1942), **Undercurrent** (1946), **Quo Vadis** (1951), **Valley of the Kings** (1954), **D-Day the Sixth of June** (1956), **Saddle the Wind** (1958), **Killers of Kilimanjaro** (1960) and **Johnny Tiger** (1966).

Divorced from Barbara Stanwyck in 1951 he had been remarried to actress Ursula Thiess in 1954. He did his last film work overseas in 1968 and died of lung cancer the next year at the age of 57.

Lt. Robert Taylor (right) serving as a Navy flight instructor in WW II. (Credit: Campbell Archives)

PAUL W. TIBBETS

Born in 1915, Paul Tibbets was a B-17 pilot in the Eighth Air Force and participated in early air raids over Europe form England. He later flew combat in North Africa and was highly decorated for these missions.

In 1944 he trained and led the 509th Composite Group of the Army Air Force at Wendover Field, Utah.

In May 1945 his group flew their B-29 Superfortress aircraft from the United States to Tinian Island in the Marianas. This unit had been especially trained in the technique for delivering an atomic bomb on target, a technique developed by Tibbets. After playing a role in the target selection Tibbets piloted the B-29 "Enola Gay" in dropping the first atomic bomb, "Little Boy," on Hiroshima, Japan on August 6, 1945.

Col. Paul Tibbets waves from the cockpit window of his B-29, "Enola Gay". The nose of the aircraft is now on display at the National Air and Space Museum in Washington, DC. (Credit: Don Spry)

Col. Paul Tibbetts receives the Distinguished Service Cross after his historic flight, 6 August 1945. (Credit: Don Spry)

Brig. Gen. Paul W. Tibbetts. (Credit: Don Spry)

A second atomic bomb was delivered by the 509th and dropped on Nagasaki on August 9, 1945. It is widely believed by World War II historians that the Japanese would not have surrendered unless the A-bombs had been dropped.

He retired from the Air Force with the rank of brigadier general.

GEORGE C. WALLACE

Born on August 24, 1919 in Clio, Alabama, a farmers son, he rose to become the governor of his state. He attended the University of Alabama and received his law degree there in 1942.

Sgt. George Wallace is shown here kneeling, third from the left with the crew of the B-29 Superfortress that they flew from the U.S. to Tinian, the Mariana Islands in 1945. (Credit: Governor George Wallace)

Governor George Wallace. (Credit: Gov. George Wallace)

That same year he enlisted in the Army Air Force for pilot training. However, a bout of meningitis forced him to abandon that training. He later became a flight engineer and served on a Twentieth Air Force B-29 flying eleven combat missions over Japan. He was honorably discharged in 1945 with the rank of sergeant and was awarded the Air Medal.

Returning to Alabama he became involved in Democratic politics and was elected to the state legislature were he became renowned for his eloquent oratory. He was elected a circuit judge in 1953 and served in that capacity until 1959. At national conventions of the Democratic Party he became known for his opposition to Civil Rights issues. He was defeated in a try for the Alabama governorship in 1958 and in November 1962 he won that office running as a segregationist.

On June 11, 1963 Wallace, flying in the face of a national desegregation movement, won prime time TV for personally barring the path of two Negro students attempting to register at the University of Alabama. As a result of this defiance President John F. Kennedy issued an executive order federalizing the Alabama National Guard and ordered them on campus to permit the registrations. Another integration crisis prompted by Wallace followed with Birmingham schools, and the National Guard was federalized (that time by President Kennedy) forcing Wallace to back down.

Continuing as a vociferous spokesman for states rights, he ran for the Democratic presidential nomination in 1968. While at an outdoor rally in Maryland he was the victim of an assassin. A bullet, lodged in his spine, crippled him for life and he has been confined to a wheel chair from that time.

BUD WILKINSON

Born in Minnesota, as Charles Wilkinson in 1916, he attended prep school at Shattuck Military Academy, Fairbault, Minnesota and then graduated from the University of Minnesota where he was an athletic standout in football, golf and hockey. He was captain of the golf team and played goalie on the hockey club. He received a B.A. in English and received his Masters Degree in English from Syracuse.

He took a job as assistant football coach at Syracuse University and served there between 1937-1940 when he moved to Minnesota.

"The Coach", Bud Wilkinson. (Credit: University of Oklahoma Archives)

With the outbreak of World War II, Wilkinson joined the Navy and received a commission as ensign. Initially he was assigned to coaching duties at the Iowa Pre-flight Navy program. However, in 1944 he served aboard the aircraft carrier *Enterprise* during the invasions of Iwo Jima, Okinawa and raids on the Japanese home islands.

Returning from the war he joined the University of Oklahoma football coaching staff in 1946 at the invitation of head coach, Jim Tatum. When Tatum left to accept a job at Maryland, Bud became the Sooner's thirteenth head coach.

During 17 years in that position his teams won 145 games, lost 29 and tied four, an 83.8 percent winning average. Wilkinson held the Oklahoma and Big Eight record for number of victories until those marks were erased by his successor, Barry Switzer. Wilkinson still ranks eighth in winning percentage among the nations Division I coaches with at least ten years of service.

He died in 1994.

TED WILLIAMS

The "Splendid Splinter", as some sports reporter nick named the lanky slugger, was born in 1918 in San Diego as Theodore Samuel Williams.

He joined the Boston Red Sox of the American League in 1939 and in 1941 he batted for an incredible .406 average.

At the peak of his fame in 1942, Williams left the Sox to answer the call to the colors. He enlisted in the U.S. Navy and joined its aviation flight program. He won his wings and his commission in the Marines

Ted Williams as a Marine flyer. (Credit: National Baseball Museum, Cooperstown, NY)

and was assigned to duty as an instructor. He returned to baseball after his honorable release in 1946. However, he retained his reserve status and his flying proficiency.

Returning to the Bosox "The Thumper" tore up American League pitching for the next six years, then another international conflict intervened and Williams was recalled to duty at age 33.

The Korean war brought him back to the Marines in 1952. He reported for duty with VMF-311, where Major John Glenn was operations officer. Jerry Coleman, a Yankee ball player was another squadronmate. Williams was forced to crash land his Grumman F9F Panther jet at an airbase after being hit by enemy anti-aircraft fire. Despite chronic pneumonia and an inner-ear problem, he completed his combat tour. He retired from active duty as a major.

Returning once again to major league baseball, for a partial season in 1953, he put in another eight years

Ted Williams, Boston's "Splendid Splinter". (Credit: Boston Red Sox)

defending the outfield and batting for Boston. He retired in 1960 with the most impressive statistics: a lifetime batting average of .344 and 521 homeruns. He only appeared in one World Series, 1946. He was inducted into the Baseball Hall of Fame in 1966.

Ted took a turn at managing in the American League, first with Washington for three seasons, and then with Texas for 1972.

CHUCK YEAGER

"The fastest man on earth", as he came to be known, was born Charles E. Yeager in West Virginia on February 13, 1923. He had just graduated from high school when he enlisted in the Army Air force and went through pilot training. He won his wings and was commissioned a flight officer in March 1943 and assigned to the 363rd Fighter Squadron, 357th Fighter Group, then training at Tonopah, Nevada.

Equipped with the North American P-51 Mustang, the group was sent to England joining the Eighth Air Force. Yeager was highly regarded for his piloting skill and scored his first victory over a German opponent near Berlin on March 4, 1944. The very next day in a fight near German airfields his plane received a fatal cannon hit, and Yeager was seen to parachute into Southern France.

Listed as "missing in action', he evaded capture, and with the help of the underground he crossed into Spain. There he was arrested and jailed, sawed his way to freedom and eventually made his way back to Allied control. Slated to be returned to the States (policy would not allow airmen who had escaped to return to combat), he argued his case all the way to the supreme commander, General Dwight Eisenhower, requesting that he be allowed to return to his outfit and continue the war, an argument he eventually won.

Returning to combat in October 1944, Yeager racked up another 10 1/2 victories and was promoted to captain. After completing 64 missions and 270 combat hours he was sent back to the States having been awarded the Silver Star with one Cluster, the Distinguished Flying Cross with two Clusters, the Air Medal with six Clusters, the Bronze Star and Purple Heart.

In the postwar years he married his sweetheart Glennis Faye Dickhouse, became a test pilot, rose in rank to major, and was assigned to the Air Force Flight Test Center, Edwards AFB, Muroc, California. Test flying the rocket-propelled Bell X-1, an experimental aircraft designed specifically to probe the deadly zone of speed that created compressibility, Yeager constantly pushed through the sonic barrier of 720 miles per hour. During a test hop on October 14, 1947 he exceeded 1,000 miles per hour. The results of these experiments were initially kept secret, shared only with the U.S. builders of military aircraft.

Yeager later test flew a captured Mig-15 and performed an array of training and research assignments retiring from the Air Force in the 1970s. It was not until well after his test pilot achievements that the full story was disclosed, so he became a celebrity to the majority of Americans in the 1980s. He retired from the Air Force in the rank of brigadier general.

His fame brought him speaking engagements and opportunities as a product sponsor on television commercials where his face and "good old boy" appearance made him a known to the general public.

Flight Officer Chuck Yeager in June 1944 on his return from months of evasion. Ike's orders returning him to his unit and flying staus are in this right pocket. (Credit: Overstreet via Merle Olmsted.)

Chuck Yeager (right) on the movie set of The Right Stuff, stands in front of the X-1 in which he gained the title, *Fastest Man Alive*. (Credit: Film Favorites